37653005294023
Main NonFict`
B FAULK`
Thinking
Faulkner
mother a`

✓

AUG 9 5

CENTRAL ARKANSAS LIBRARY SYSTEM
LITTLE ROCK PUBLIC LIBRARY
LITTLE ROCK, ARKANSAS

THINKING
OF HOME

CENTRAL ARKANSAS LIBRARY SYSTEM
LITTLE ROCK PUBLIC LIBRARY
LITTLE ROCK, ARKANSAS

THINKING
OF HOME

*William
Faulkner's
Letters to
His Mother
and Father
1918 - 1925*

Edited by
JAMES G. WATSON

W·W·Norton & Company
New York   London

94-20542

CENTRAL ARKANSAS LIBRARY SYSTEM
LITTLE ROCK PUBLIC LIBRARY
LITTLE ROCK, ARKANSAS

Copyright © 1992 by James G. Watson
Letters Copyright © 1992 by W. W. Norton & Company, Inc.
All rights reserved.
Printed in the United States of America.
The text of this book is composed in
11.5/14 Bodoni Book,
with the display set in
Typositor Radiant Bold Condensed & Bodoni Book Italic
Composition and manufacturing by the
Haddon Craftsmen, Inc.
Book design by Margaret M. Wagner.

First Edition.

Library of Congress Cataloging in Publication Data
Faulkner, William, 1897 1962.
Thinking of home : William Faulkner's letters to his
mother and
father, 1918–1925 / edited by James G. Watson.
p. cm.
Includes index.
1. Faulkner, William, 1897–1962—Correspondence. 2.
Faulkner,
William, 1897–1962—Biography—Family. 3. Novelists,
American—20th
century—Biography—Family. 4. Novelists,
American—20th century—
Correspondence. I. Watson, James G. (James Gray),
1939–
II. Title.
PS3511.A86Z48 1992
813'.52—dc20
[B]   91–16283

ISBN 0-393-03081-4

W. W. Norton & Company, Inc.
500 Fifth Avenue, New York, N.Y. 10110
W.W. Norton & Company Ltd.
10 Coptic Street, London WCIA 1PU

1 2 3 4 5 6 7 8 9 0

For my parents,
William G. Watson and
Margaret M. Watson, and for
Ruth Dye Boyles

Contents

Acknowledgments

THE letters of William Faulkner to his mother and father, 1912 and 1918–1925, are published with the kind permission of Jill Faulkner Summers, and of the Harry Ransom Humanities Research Center, the University of Texas at Austin, whose director, Dr. Thomas F. Staley, initiated the project with me and gave it his unwavering support. Here as elsewhere I have enjoyed the benefit of his firm friendship and wise counsel. I am indebted to Professors Joseph L. Blotner and Warwick Wadlington, who read the letters with me, to Thomas L. McHaney, who read the manuscript, and to Thomas Bonner, Norman Grabo and Gordon O. Taylor, who read and advised me on parts of it. At the HRHRC, John Chalmers, Cathy Henderson, Chris Kiesling, and John Kirkpatrick gave me the substantive benefit of their archival and manuscript expertise. Many others there volunteered their help, among them Linda Ashton, Ruth Bartell, Ken Cravens, Dr. Raymond Daum, Dr. Carlton Lake, Sally Leach, Sue Murphy, James Stroud, and Richard B. Watson. By a happy coincidence, the Carvel Collins Collection of William Faulkner became available at HRHRC as I was beginning this project, and I have made generous use of information about Faulkner therein. In Tulsa, Kimberley Nicolas helped with the annotations, and Mrs. Russell Pigford talked with me about New Orleans in the mid-1920s. I am pleased to acknowledge the additional assistance of the Yale University Office of Public Information and the New

10 / ACKNOWLEDMENTS

Haven Colonial Historical Society. The University of Tulsa made available time to write and the Tulsa Faculty Research Program provided some funds for travel. Though they cannot read this book, Yvonne Blotner and Michael Whalon were important to its making from the beginning.

James G. Watson
Tulsa, Oklahoma

Introduction

*"How often have I lain beneath rain on a
strange roof, thinking of home."—As I Lay
Dying*

IN the spring of 1918, William Faulkner left Oxford, Mississippi, for a ten-week stay in New Haven, Connecticut, with his friend Phil Stone. He was twenty years old. It was his first extended absence from home. Thus began an extensive correspondence with his mother and father that continued on succeeding trips through 1925: to Canada with the Royal Air Force (July to December 1918); to New Haven and New York (October to December 1921); to New Orleans and the Gulf Coast (January to July 1925); and to Europe (August to December 1925). His 145 letters, postcards, and telegrams to his parents from the first four of those trips, and from the last six weeks of his European journey, are published here for the first time, with his earliest extant letter, from Oxford in 1912. They are the letters of a young man coming of age. Overflowing with the stuff of his everyday life, they range from outpourings of feeling for his "Darling Momsey" to more confident self-representations of the dutiful son. The majority precede but look forward to Faulkner's earliest sense of himself as a serious artist; those from New Orleans and Europe in 1925 trace his intellectual and imaginative awakening as a first novelist. As a group, they provide a picture of Faulkner at a time in his life about which less has been known than any other.

Thinking of Home

WRITING to his mother about Oxford war casualties late in 1918, Faulkner found it "queer" that those who loved their homes most had been the first to enlist and so leave them. Then he qualified that judgment. "It isnt so queer, though," he wrote, "for only he whose heart and soul is wrapped about his home can see the utterly worthless but human emotions such as selfishness, and know that home is the thing worth having above everything, and it is well known that what is not worth fighting for is not worth having." As the many related letters show, this romantic letter to his mother is less about protecting home than it is about regaining it. He wrote, ". . . when its all over and Jack and I are back again and we are sitting around the table at night, we'll go back about ten years and start living there, for even though we are both objective kids now, I can—and Jackie too—realize that home is greater that [sic] war, or lightening or marriage or any other unavoidable thing." Faulkner was then a Royal Air Force cadet-pilot stationed in Canada, but his letter does more than express the understandable nostalgia of a homesick recruit. It reconstitutes the temporarily forfeited home as an element in a seamless history and, by reconnecting the letter writer's future to his past, heals the present rupture in his life.

Personal letters are generated by such absences, which they attempt to overcome. They reach out across geographical distances to span separations between correspondents and assert relationship. Letters conventionally address a "dear" receiver and convey the sender's best wishes, sincerity, or love. In this way, a letter literally depicts both the receiver (or reader) and the sender (or writer), affirming the relationship it defines between them by joining their separate images on the page. A letter is the surrogate of the writer. Figuratively as well as literally, it places his or her "hand" into the reader's.

It is because of such biographical and autobiographical presentations of writer and reader that correspondents save each other's personal letters, and it is for this reason that they are published. In the case of the present volume of William Faulkner's correspondence with his mother and father, the letters document for the first time places he visited and lived during the period 1918–1925, events in which he took part, and people he met. They say what he felt and thought, what pleased or disappointed him, what he hoped, delighted in, and feared. Because they do these things, the letters offer a version of his life at that time—presented, it is important to remember, from his own perspective and always, in the case of this collection, in the specific context of his relationship to his mother and to his father. Those relationships necessarily were somewhat different, especially with regard to letters and letter-writing, and they are differently represented in the collection. Nonetheless, together Faulkner's letters to Maud and to Murry Falkner represent strands of his most deep-felt ties to a nurturing and sustaining home. There, as later in his fiction, home defined him. Absent from home periodically during his early and middle twenties, he conceived of it as both a place and an idea in letters whose frequency and individual intensities testify to the strength of the home-bond.

Faulkner's absences from Oxford from 1918 to 1925, as later, were temporary ones, but he wrote home regularly and often. The shortest of the five periods away was seven weeks in 1921, the longest nearly twelve months in 1925. During all of these periods he wrote home no less often on average than once every five days. And his own letters generated responses: he speculated that he received more mail in Canada than anyone else in his squadron. His letters to his mother evoke home especially in terms of food, clothing, children, and childhood memories. He praises her cooking, compares Northern to Southern foods, and prepares imaginary menus of meals he will eat when he comes home. "No," he wrote her from Paris in October 1925, "I'll have to admit I dont have sweet potatoes, nor fresh ham nor hot biscuits either—though I am to soon." In turn she sent him cakes and cookies, knitted the sweaters and socks he requested, and made dress shirts and sleeve liners according to his written specifications. To her he sent small gifts for his younger brothers Johnsy and Dean and for Mammy Callie Barr, inquired after friends and family, and reminisced about the past. Several of his letters are illustrated with sophisticated line drawings, some of which are portraits of himself; several contained photographs. Only in letters to his mother did he speak of his art.

To his father he wrote far less often and in different terms. Murry Falkner had been a railroader and owned a livery stable and hardware store before he became assistant secretary of the University of Mississippi, and Faulkner wrote him detailed descriptions of trains and reported visiting "one of the largest hardware houses in America." Murry was far less a letter writer than Maud. Yet he did write to his son, and the three letters Faulkner wrote him and the nineteen in which he addressed Maud and Murry together are loving, considerate, and equally concerned with home. In contrast to his letters to his mother, Faulkner wrote to his father about Southern ways and Mississippi landscapes. He reported on racial attitudes in the North, often critically in ways that Murry would have approved. Letters to Murry, and nearly every reference to him in letters to Maud, involve an outdoor setting or activity—Woodson's Ridge in the autumn, squirrel hunting along the Pontotoc Road, tramping misty fields behind the university. Clearly, he thought of his father in physical rather than intellectual terms. He was ironic about Murry's appointment to the university administration in 1918 and pleased in 1925 when his father had to moderate his work. "Its too bad dad must give up an old and comfortable habit," he wrote in April 1925, "but I am glad the doctor is making him stay away from that office. There is too much in the world to see, to spend all the time between four walls."

Home is implicit in Faulkner's reports of people and events he encountered on his travels—in a chance meeting with a stranger from Georgia who recognized his Mississippi accent, or with friends from home such as Rufus Creekmore in New Haven and Harry Rainold and Russell Pigford in New Orleans. A newsboy in Toronto and a wanderer in New Orleans remind him of his youngest brother, Dean; Marjorie Gumbel's baby girl recalls his infant nephew Jimmy. Home was the standard of his every judgment: "Dad would be crazy about this country," he wrote from Canada, "everything is so pretty now, almost as colorful as our falls, and it lasts so much longer." He wrote from New Orleans in the spring of 1925, "golly, I miss the hills and fruit trees and things now." To both parents he commented on news they sent him of home, and his letters are filled with names of local friends and acquaintances—Ed Beanland, who died in the war, Edison Avent, who was rejected for service, Sonny Bell, who succeeded Faulkner as university postmaster, and the Mississippian in Canada who knew all the boys from Meridian. Others he did not identify—among them Dr. Lawhon, Brad Farmer and Uncle George, and "Toc" Whitehead, Van Hiler, Roselle, and Mat. Homecoming is his constant theme, anticipated in scenes as different as the family table with his brothers and the local golf course with Dr. Rowland, Prof. Torrey, and Dr. Bell. "Oh, boy," he wrote his mother near the end of his R.A.F. service in 1918, "but I mean I'm coming home. I'm Alabama bound, and if I miss the train, I've got a mule to ride!"

Some Consequences of Correspondence

LIKE any substantial collection of a writer's personal papers, the previously unpublished letters from William Faulkner to his mother and father have a number of "consequences" for our understanding of his life and art. We see him here retrospectively through his own immediate impressions of himself and his foreign surroundings. Appearing as they do nearly thirty years after Faulkner's death in 1962 and nearly twenty years after the publication of the authorized biography, the letters expand the store of biographical fact about a period of Faulkner's life, and consequently will correct or enrich prior speculations and established understandings. The William Faulkner of these letters is not yet the author of the great masterworks. He is younger and less sophisticated, by turns confused and delighted by the commonplaces and the surprises of life in a university town, army camp, Eastern metropolis, artists' conclave, and European center. He is at once an adventurer in the world beyond Oxford and a dependent son, self-consciously writing himself into being.

ADVENTURER

For an untraveled young man from Oxford, Mississippi, New Haven in 1918 was a university city so unlike Oxford or even Memphis as to be an adventure in itself. His first impressions were exclusively of difference. "I had no idea there would be so much difference in the temperature" were virtually the first words he wrote to his mother. Within twenty-four hours he had noted the scarcity of theaters and movie theaters, the unusual size of locomotives, the New Haven way of measuring distance in minutes instead of miles, the inexpensive food, the remarkable phenomenon of tickertape machines, and the habits and habiliments of people his age. Of Yale students he said, "it's funny, they all drink, even the faculty members drink with them, but nobody ever gets drunk"; of their fashions in dress he wrote, "Tight clothes and pink and yellow shirts are as rare here as negroes, and—outside of the hotel staffs—I have seen one." Within the month he was asking his mother for shirts of a different kind, his design for a one-button collar enclosed. He saw former President Taft from a distance. He saw the ocean for the first time and thought it "the most wonderful thing I've seen yet," worked at his first full time job outside the Falkner family bank—at the Winchester Repeating Arms Co.—and found it agreed with him, and discovered that New Haven was multinational—and nationalistic. He learned to eat pie for breakfast, dined in a Chinese restaurant, lunched with Hindu workers at Winchester, and met "a dyed-in-the-wool Englishman" who said "awsk" instead of "ask" and "cawnt" instead of "can't." "It's funny to walk the streets and look at these people," he wrote. "Poles, Russians, Italian Communists, all with American flags in their lapels. And yet they say God made man in his own image." He mentioned his Oxford sweetheart Estelle Oldham only once, to ask about her wedding; a month later he devoted two paragraphs to a Woolworth's salesgirl he said was "as exquisite as a Dresden vase, or a figure by Tanagra." Those particular images would come back to him for years in descriptions of women and even of books.

Working during the day, and a half-day on Saturdays, reading at the Brick Row Book Shop, writing letters and playing bridge with Stone's friends in the evening, he found a new kind of excitement in every day. Of the cultural life of the university, he said very little. On weekends he and Stone explored the country outside New Haven, especially the sea-shore, or attended sporting events at Yale. He thought less of baseball than of boat races, and said of lacrosse that it was "a cross between 'skinny' and first degree murder." "La Crosse is indigent with the Indians," he explained to his mother. He kept up with the war news, too. Oxford had been a quiet backwater of the war, but New Haven was full of troops either training for overseas service or recuperating from wounds. He described their different uniforms in de-tail and their disabilities. On Decoration Day he saw planes from a base on Long Island overfly New Haven and engage in a mock dogfight, and he watched the Yale Army and Navy Corps parade, and a group of black Civil War veter-ans. "Even the Italians had a parade," he reported. "They were all short and fierce like brigands. The Chinese, for some reason, didn't have one."

In early June he wrote that he had "a chance to join up with the British and get a commission as a second lieuten-ant—leftenant they call it—in about three months after I am sent to training camp." On June 14, having secured his mother's permission, he went to New York to meet Lieuten-ant Colonel Lord Wellesley to enlist. Here the 1918 New Haven letters raise questions they leave unanswered. John Falkner would remember that his brother had tried and failed to enlist in the Aviation Section of the U.S. Army Signal Corps before going to New Haven, but Faulkner mentions only his and Jack's wanting to drive ambulances in France. Later Phil Stone would describe an elaborate plot to prove his and Faulkner's British citizenship involving forged letters of recommendation sent to England for posting there. Faulkner did have false references, as his letters show—from an Englishman named Bernard Reed, from a high school principal who had rooms with Stone, and from a professor of ancient literature who presented him as a second-year Yale man—but there was hardly time before his enlistment in mid-June to send and return mail across the Atlantic. Still more intriguing is the fact that his letters make no mention of the Royal Air Force or of Canada—this despite the fact that Lord Wellesley was the R.A.F. officer in charge of cadet recruiting in New York, and that Faulkner's friend and adviser in New Haven, though not yet a flier himself, was the Canadian Lieutenant Todd. The opportunity, as Faulkner said Todd had explained it, developed from the scarcity of British army officers to command the "two million unofficial reserve troops in house now, which they cant use at all." His account of the reasons for the shortage, if he can be believed, is as naive as his hopes for immediate advancement are optimistic. "The English officers are the best yet," he assured Maud Falkner. "So I shall learn war in the best of schools, where the elimination of risk is taught above everything."

If that specious argument was for his mother's benefit, it does not hide the fact that Faulkner was far less interested in seeing action than in seeing Europe. He expected to be trained at Oxford or Cambridge—"it will be wonderful just seeing England and those places," he wrote—and he anticipated quick promotion, perhaps to major at the end of a year's service. The present opportunity potentially had bearing on the more distant future, as well, and Faulkner's hope of that finds expression in a darker understanding of his present. "At the rate I am living now," he said at the end of his letter, "I will never be able to make anything of myself, but with this business I'll be fixed up after the war is over." In that context, the motto of the Royal Air Force, when he learned it, must have had special appeal: Per Ardua ad Astra!

SPONSORED INDEPENDENCE

The same darker note had been sounded in a different context by Phil Stone in a letter he wrote to his mother when Faulkner joined him in New Haven early in April. It generally has been understood that Faulkner left Oxford primarily to absent himself from home when Estelle married Cornell Franklin, and that was doubtless part of his motive. But Stone typically took a longer view. He wrote, in part, "I don't think he is going to be homesick. I have introduced him around to all of my friends and acquaintances, some of them rather brilliant people, and they seem to like him very much. He is a fine, intelligent little fellow and I think that he is going to amount to a lot some day; I certainly am glad that I got him away from Oxford for he was just going to seed there." Stone's sponsorship of his younger friend marks a pattern of dependency in Faulkner's journeys away from Mississippi that carried through 1925. In New Haven in 1918, Stone arranged Faulkner's job at Winchester, shared his rooms at 120 York Street, introduced him to his friends at his Corby Court law club and the Brick Row Book Shop, and conspired in his enlistment in the R.A.F. Three years later, when Faulkner came east again, Stone's friends arranged his affairs and looked after him in New Haven, and the Mississippi poet and critic Stark Young found him a job in New York and lodged him temporarily. He was taken up in New Orleans in 1925 first by Elizabeth Prall Anderson, who cooked his meals and banked his money for him, and then by her husband, Sherwood Anderson, who introduced Faulkner to the New Orleans artist colony and to visiting dignitaries, including his publisher, Horace Liveright, and

oversaw, as these letters show, both the writing and the
initial stages of publication of Faulkner's first novel, *Soldiers' Pay*. Faulkner originally had planned to leave for
Europe alone in January 1925. When he did sail in July, it
was with his New Orleans friend Bill Spratling. He assured
his mother that they would not be entirely on their own:
"Bill and I have been given by kind friends a hundred addresses of nice people in Europe who will feed us," he
wrote, adding that "a friend of Bill's is to meet us at the
dock." In Paris in November, after Spratling's departure,
Faulkner was helped through financial difficulties by Spratling's New Orleans acquaintance the photographer William
C. Odiorne.

Each of these men, being older or more experienced than
Faulkner, provided him support beyond his own immediate
resources of a kind that balanced and in some cases made
possible his otherwise solitary adventuring. And everywhere he made friends. "All these people are awfully nice to
me," he wrote from New Haven. From Toronto he wrote,
"These people are wonderful to me." Solitary Faulkner
might have been on his trips away from Oxford, but he was
seldom alone. His was a sponsored independence, and one
in which his letters to and from his home played a major
supportive part. "I couldn't live here at all," he wrote his
mother from New Haven, "but for your letters." In the
absence of visitors during R.A.F. ground school at Long
Branch, he satisfied himself with correspondence: "letters,"
he said, "are the next best thing."

In Canada the R.A.F. chain of command and the King's
Orders and Regulations made an adventurous experience so
safe for a cadet-pilot—and sometimes so dull—that he invented adventures for his parents. His subsequent accounts
of his flights and crash landings begin here, and he was
using an invented name. Faulkner added the "u" to Falkner

at the Winchester plant in New Haven and retained it when he enlisted. Now, and for the only time in his correspondence, he appropriated that spelling for his parents: thirty-two of the forty-five letters to his mother from Canada and fourteen of the fifteen to Maud and Murry together are addressed to "Mrs. M. C. Faulkner." Sometimes, the envelopes show, he added the "u" after writing "Falkner." Such inventions are grounded in a correspondence as remarkable for the letters it generated from home as for its own scope and breadth. Faulkner's niece reports that Maud Falkner insisted her sons write her every week when they were away, and Faulkner promises that in an early letter from Europe in 1925. In the twenty-two weeks between his R.A.F. enlistment on July 8 and his demobilization in late December, however, he wrote to his parents an average of once every two and a half days. References in his letters to Maud and Murry indicate that he also wrote or mailed packages to his brothers Jack, Johnsy, and Dean, to his grandfather, to various aunts and cousins, and to friends such as Phil Stone and Katrina Carter. Midway through his Canadian stay, he lamented, "As for writing often, I wish I had more time to write you all." He received letters from all of these as well as packages from his mother that contained four cakes, three hand-knitted sweaters, socks, books, magazines, cigarettes, candy, a towel, toothpaste, jelly, cheese, and a pair of leather leggings he was not allowed to wear until he was commissioned. "I have gotten more mail lately than anyone in the camp or the Flying Corps, for that matter," he wrote early in August. "I average about 4 a day, and one of my tent mates, a chap who transferred from the Army Service Corps, said, Gee, Faulkner, some one is certainly in love with you. And I told him that some one was, two for that matter."

His support from home included money, as well—in

Canada nearly three-quarters of the amount he was paid at the cadet-pilot rate of $1.10 a day. As he did throughout his travels at this time, he appears to have taken that financial support for granted. Near the end of his R.A.F. service, he wrote Maud that he needed $30 for a coat and to pay a dentist, but added, "I don't want to ask, for I have gotten along so far without having to go begging. I know that you and Dad would be glad to do anything for me, which is the reason I dont want to ask." To that point they had sent him at least $60. His $60 fare home was paid by his father. When he arrived he had managed to replace the authorized cadet uniform issued him in Toronto with the tailored tunic and breeches of an R.A.F. second lieutenant he purchased after the Armistice.

THE ARTIST AS A YOUNG MAN

Faulkner submitted poetry for publication from New Haven in 1918, and sent his mother poems from Canada, but the sense of artistic vocation that pervades his letters from New Orleans and Europe at the middle of the decade emerges strongly for the first time in the letters of 1921. He went east in October of that year to make himself a writer, and passages from his letters then are as imaginative and beautiful as any in his correspondence. Typically, his first response was to the physical landscape of New England and his memory of it. The day he arrived in New Haven he wrote Maud Falkner:

There's only one sensation to be compared with seeing mountains, and that's seeing the ocean again. Coming up along the sound yesterday I was looking for it all the time; there's a strange feeling in the air: you pass through tight little New England villages built around plots of grass they call greens. The sky toward the sea is pale, about the color of salt, against which the inevitable white church spires are drawn clearer and whiter still. Every where the trees are turning—fall has already come here—ferns, and gum trees, all the underbrush is yellow and red, and over the whole thing is a queer feeling, an awareness of the slow magnificent ocean, like something you have heard or smelled, and forgotten. Then, suddenly, you see it, a blue hill going up and up, beyond the borders of the world, to the salt colored sky, and white whirling necklaces of gulls, and, if you look long enough, a great vague ship solemnly going some where. I cant express how it makes me feel to see it again, there is a feeling of the most utter relief, as if I could close my eyes, knowing that I had found again someone who loved me years and years ago.

Subsequent letters written from New England that fall describe New Haven scenes with the same consciousness of imaginative effect. One contained a landscape and a seascape done in crayon, the only two such pieces Faulkner is known to have done.

Unemployed, he was in New Haven specifically to write, and his letters range between imaginative intensities and languid descriptions of his days in the familiar university town. New York, conversely, was a city of speed, as exciting as it was overwhelming in its complexity. A week after arriving he wrote:

This town is certainly a wonderful place to be as unpleasant. It's too darned crowded for me ever to like it, but as for possessing means of going from one place to another in a hurry, there's nothing to compare with it. I live about ten miles from Mr Stark, yet I can nip down a hole in the ground, take a subway to the Grand Central Terminal, take a shuttle train from there without ever seeing day light, go to Times Square and—still without coming into the world, take another train and pop up out of a hole at Mr Stark's door, all for a nickle. It's marvelous, but you're just like a rat.

In New York he spoke of art school, and of supporting himself with his drawings while he wrote, but he stayed less than three weeks.

In New Orleans in 1925 he was at once more sure of himself and more at home. His letters document a schedule of writing that produced the series of sketches he sold to the *Times-Picayune*, poems and essays published in the *Double-Dealer*, and several stories and reviews. Imaginatively he was at such a pitch that his fiction writing carried into his letters. He had to assure his mother that some of the adventures he recounted were real. Others, like an encounter with a writing school representative, almost certainly were inventions. Yet invention, as always with Faulkner, spilled out of experience. "What really happens," he confided, "never makes a good yarn. You have got to get an impulse from somewhere and then embroider it." In New Orleans in 1925 a primary "impulse" derived from his Canadian service: a letter of February 16 contains the first announcement of his first novel, *Soldiers' Pay.* "Right now I am 'thinking out' a novel," he said. "As soon as I get it all straight, I will begin work." Work on the book coincided with Sherwood Anderson's arrival in the city in early March. Faulkner announced then, "Sherwood and I are writing a book together," and he closed by detailing his writing schedule. "I am writing a novel of my own, helping Sherwood write our mutual book, beside my Chartres street series. They start again next sunday, I think. I also wrote today an article on 'What is wrong with marriage?' for the Times. In fact, I have more stuff than I can get time to write." Starting in April his letters detail his progress with the book that would be *Soldiers' Pay:* they help us to understand his way of working as they also correct misconceptions about its composition. On May 12 he reported, "I finished my novel last night. I think I wrote almost 10000 words yesterday between 10:00 AM and midnight." As he worked on revising and retyping the book and planned for his European trip, his letters to his mother faltered for the first time from their regular schedule. "I'm sorry I slipped up about writing," he wrote her from Pascagoula in late June. "But when you spend most of your time writing words, as long as you are all right you want to take it out in thinking about home—writing letters is like the postman taking a long walk on his day off."

The eleven letters from Paris and New York that complete the published record of his European trip in 1925 are the work of a self-assured artist. As usual, Faulkner was busy with several projects at once—the novels *Elmer* and *Mosquitoes* and a group of stories that had grown to seven by November 21. A year earlier, before he went to New Orleans, Phil Stone had arranged for his book of poems to be published by a vanity press. Now, with a contract for his first novel from Boni & Liveright, and promises for the next two, he was ready to return home to get on with his life as a writer. Significantly, it was not his mother but his father to whom he wrote in October to say that his wandering was over and his future assured.

I returned to Paris today and found your letter. I have just been thinking myself that I have been away from our blue hills and sage fields and things long enough. So I am making arrangements to come home. I will wait here for a short time because I am expecting to hear from the publisher, Mr Liveright. But I'll be on the way soon. I have plenty of notes and data to last me a long time: all I need now is to settle down at home comfortable again and bang my typewriter.

Personal Distances: Letters and Fictions

THE self-invention characteristic of letter-writing is the twin of artistic creation, and the 1918–1925 letters dramatically affirm that for Faulkner the two were inextricably intertwined. Distanced by time and context, personal experiences described in the letters crossed into his novels and stories; and sometimes inventions in the letters became "facts" of his life. Ten years after describing adventures in New Haven, Faulkner wrote specifics of them into *The Sound and the Fury.* A decade and a half after that, he assured his nephew, on the eve of his service as a Marine pilot, of the literal truth of flying experiences he had invented in letters from Canada in 1918.

What Faulkner's letters do not contain is specifics of his developing aesthetic understanding. He might send Maud Falkner his poems and stories, describe the arrangement of pictures in the Metropolitan Museum, and sketch the plot of his novel, but nowhere does he share with her details about his reading, the plays he saw and music heard, or the conversations he had with artists he met. What books he read during afternoons at the Brick Row Book Shop in New Haven or borrowed from friends in New Orleans must be gathered from other sources than his letters to his mother. Despite her own interest in art and her support of his writing, she was not a correspondent with whom he shared ideas. His interest in Joyce, Eliot, and Aiken, the intellectual life of New Haven and Yale during his stays there, plays he might have seen in New York with Stark Young—none of that is recorded in his letters to his mother. In New Orleans, other sources suggest, he first read Sigmund Freud, Sir James Frazer's *The Golden Bough,* and Havelock Ellis's

Studies in the Psychology of Sex. An unpublished letter to Sherwood Anderson in 1925 reports on his reading R. H. Mottram's *The Spanish Farm*, which he reviewed with work by Siegfried Sassoon and Henri Barbusse that spring; *Soldiers' Pay* and *Mosquitoes* are storehouses of literary, philosophical, and psychological allusion; but all of this that Faulkner communicated to his mother is summed up in his account of an evening with the New Orleans poet and book critic John McClure in 1925.

> Everyone here is grand to me—painters and writers, etc. A young painter is calling formally upon me tomorrow, and Sunday I am to dine with one of the literary arbiters of New Orleans. Last night I had dinner with John McClure, a poet and literary editor of the the Times-Picayune—by the way, he has reviewed my book [*The Marble Faun*], next Sunday it will appear, I suppose—and we talked and sipped hot whiskey punch until daylight, then walked down to the river to see the sun rise.

The value of the letters to Faulkner's literary achievement lies elsewhere, in part in the literary uses to which he put experiences he first wrote about to Maud and Murry Falkner. With distancing, immediate impressions inscribed in his letters became the stuff of fictional immediacy. The letters were a written record of personal experiences real and imagined, an archival resource of characters, places, names, dates, settings, and events potentially available to be incorporated into fiction—whether he ever reread them or not. In his war stories of the 1920s, his portrayal of the Indian subadar of "Ad Astra" derives from Hindu workers Faulkner knew at the Winchester plant in New Haven and an Indian roommate in Toronto named Durla Bushell. A shell-shocked British officer in New Haven provided the name Bland in "Ad Astra," and the Yale law student Karl Nickerson (or Nicholas) Llewellyn, who had studied in Germany before the war and who Faulkner said had served eight months in the German army, is the likely impulse for the German defector in that story. A scene in the story "Victory," in which Alec Gray is sent to a penal battalion for failing to shave, was inspired by Faulkner's being put on report for the same reason in Toronto. In *Soldiers' Pay*, Cadet Lowe and the wounded Major Donald Mahon share in real disappointments and imagined adventures that Cadet-Pilot Faulkner first recorded in letters from Canada in 1918.

The debt of *The Sound and the Fury* to the New Haven and Canadian letters is more comprehensive and, given the stature of that book, more important. Especially this is so of the second chapter, "June Second, 1910," set at Harvard, in which Faulkner's autobiographical protagonist Quentin Compson prepares to commit suicide by drowning. Insistent attempts to demonstrate that by 1928 Faulkner knew Cambridge and Harvard well enough to write about it in detail have so far produced no hard evidence of his having been there. His letters from New Haven, conversely, testify to the extent of his imaginative extension of personal into fictional experience, and support the contrary view that Quentin's Harvard is Faulkner's Yale. Quentin's concern to wear a hat, the letters show, derives from the Yale tradition then allowing only seniors to go bareheaded. The surnames of Quentin's adversary, Gerald Bland, and of Caddy's husband, Herbert Head, originate in a letter from New Haven describing Captain Bland and the Brick Row Book Shop poet Arthur Head. The character Deacon in the novel appears to be a compound of the black lay minister Blind Jim, a fixture on the University of Mississippi campus, and a black man Faulkner saw in a Decoration Day parade in New Haven. Even the dates coincide. On June 2, 1918, Faulkner wrote his mother:

> The colored troops were there, veterans of the civil war, dolled up in blue suits and cigars and medals until they all looked like brigadiers.
>
> When the veterans passed, a fellow named DeLacey who was watching the parade said to me—"Well, Bill, you ought to salute the old boys. It was your grandfather and his friends who put him that way." I told him that I thought they should salute me, for had it not been for my grandfather and his friends they would not have had any war to go to. Even the Italians had a parade, including one nigger with an Italian flag and a cigar.

Ten years later, in *The Sound and the Fury*, Faulkner placed Deacon in both parades. Like Blind Jim, Deacon is a minister—a self-avowed graduate of Harvard Divinity School—with special responsibility for freshmen students from the South. On the fictional June 2, 1910, Quentin remembers seeing Deacon "on Decoration Day, in a G.A.R. uniform, in the middle of the parade," and he recalls a previous occasion, "Columbus' or Garibaldi's or somebody's birthday. He was in the Street Sweepers' section, in a stovepipe hat, carrying a two inch Italian flag, smoking a cigar among the brooms and scoops." Faulkner's exchange with Al DeLacey was written into the novel, revised, as an exchange between Quentin and his Harvard roommate, the Canadian Shreve McKenzie.

> "There now," [Shreve said]. "Just look at what your grandpa did to that poor old nigger."
>
> "Yes," I said. "Now he can spend day after day marching in

parades. If it hadn't been for my grandfather, he'd have to
work like whitefolks."

The coalescence of an individual familiar to him from the
Mississippi campus with the image of a man glimpsed in a
New Haven street produced in Deacon a singular fictional
character whose complexity permits Quentin to see in the
contexts of the novel what Faulkner did not say in his letter—Quentin sees the true man "behind all his whitefolks'
claptrap of uniforms and politics and Harvard manner, dif-
fident, secret, inarticulate and sad." The humorous moment
from the letter is not forgotten in the novel but thematically
enriched; it was supported, as Faulkner reconstituted his
experience at New Haven and Yale, by other insights and
situations first recorded in the letters.

In New Haven and in his dormitory room at the University of Toronto, Faulkner repeatedly described scenes seen
from his window as Quentin does in *The Sound and the
Fury*. In his June 2 letter, he wrote that he and Stone had
ridden a trolley nine miles to Derby the previous day to see
the boat races that Quentin remembers on June 2, 1910, will
be held at New London. Their return trip from Derby
echoes in the novel in Quentin's solitary, troubled return
from the country by train and street car: "It took us three
hours to get back," Faulkner said of the ride back to town.
"Never had such an uncomfortable trip in my life." Quentin's purchase of flatirons to weight himself down in the
water is explained by a suggestive passage in the same letter
in which Faulkner describes swimming in the ocean for the
first time: "I dont see how anyone ever drowns in the sea,"
he said. "You can float like a cigar box."

Finally, the personal distances between Faulkner's letters
and fiction may reflect his own unstated states of mind and
emotions which extend, in *The Sound and the Fury*, to

letters themselves. Quentin lacks the sustaining correspondence at Harvard that sponsored Faulkner's independence at Yale and later—especially his correspondence with Maud Faulkner, to whom he wrote, "I couldn't live here at all but for your letters. I love you darling." Quentin's last day is filled with letters, both real and imagined, but the only letter he receives from home is the taunting wedding invitation that he hardly can bring himself to read. Near the end of his day, and his life, Quentin cries out to himself, "if I'd just had a mother so I could say Mother Mother."

The Harry Ransom Humanities Research Center Collection, The University of Texas at Austin

THE Harry Ransom Humanities Research Center Collection of William Faulkner's letters to his family contains 140 letters, four telegrams, and two postcards. A census of the collection shows that 117 letters, two telegrams, and two postcards are to Maud Falkner, three letters and two telegrams to Murry, nineteen letters to Maud and Murry together, and one letter to Faulkner's youngest brother, Dean. In these figures, letters addressed to one parent with salutations to both are counted as letters to both; letters without salutation are counted according to the name of the addressee on the envelope. The one letter without envelope or salutation is counted as a letter to Maud on the basis of internal evidence. One letter to Maud Falkner contains a carbon of a letter to Mr. R. E. Little. One hundred nineteen of the letters and postcards are handwritten, in pencil and/or ink; of the twenty-three typed letters, twenty-two are from New Orleans and one from Paris. All but twenty-two of the letters have postmarked envelopes. The letters themselves are written variously on folded note paper, on embossed stationery of the R.A.F. and random other places, on standard 8½-by-11-inch manuscript paper, and on what is apparently journalist's paper marked with broad blue or red margins at the left and top of the page. Probably none of the five groupings from 1918 to 1925 includes every letter Faulkner wrote to his parents during the period. References in the collection to letters not found there are frequent enough to suggest either that Maud and Murry never received them or that they did not save them with the rest. One letter from Canada in 1918 and the first half of Faulkner's European correspondence with his parents, from August through mid-October 1925, are in the Jill Faulkner Summers Archive and have been published in *Selected Letters of William Faulkner*.

In preparing this edition of Faulkner's correspondence, I have attempted to produce a reasonable approximation of his letter page. None of the Humanities Research Center letters is a polished manuscript. Faulkner sometimes wrote to his parents hurriedly as well as regularly, and his idiosyncrasies as a letter writer often are accompanied by errors of haste. Most but by no means all of the letters have salutations and signatures; only the European letters are consistently dated with more than the day of the week. In holograph and typewritten letters, sentences and clauses ending at the right margin frequently are not punctuated and words broken at the right margin are not hyphenated. Initial words in sentences are not always capitalized, nor are place-names: Faulkner may write "dad" for "Dad," "st." for "St.," "Hudson bay" for "Hudson Bay." Contractions sometimes have the apostrophe and sometimes not: he may write "Ill" for "I'll" or "wouldnt" for "wouldn't"; he never uses the apostrophe with single-syllable contractions such as "cant," "wont," and "aint." Compound words may be hyphenated ("to-morrow") or written as separate words (to night," "some where"), and either or both forms may appear with the standard usage in the same letter or even the same sentence. The family name on envelopes of letters from Canada usually is spelled "Faulkner," with a "u," and an inquiry from his mother answered by Lieutenant Colonel Wellesley indicates that she probably wrote to her son as Faulkner, as well.

Except in the cases noted below, Faulkner's usage has been retained. Cancellations are indicated as such and where recoverable they are transcribed. Illegible cancellations are indicated as such within brackets: [illegible]. A few uncertain readings are given in brackets with a question mark: [Yule ?]. Strikeovers and revisions of false starts or errors in spelling are transcribed in the revised form only. Spelling errors are retained. Repeated words, as at the ends and beginnings of lines or pages, have been silently deleted; the position of quotation marks with punctuation has been regularized. The designation [sic] is used only in the rare instances where confusion of meaning might otherwise result. Illustrations in the texts of the letters are indicated by [FIGURE] and a descriptive footnote. Significant names, places, dates, and events are identified in footnotes when such information is available.

The letters are arranged chronologically and numbered by section. The name of the addressee, as indicated by his or her name on an envelope [env], a telegram [telegram], or postcard [postcard], is given with the date or postmark, the place of origin, and the salutation, if any:

To Mrs. M. C. Falkner   Friday [19 July 1918]
[env]   [Toronto]

Dear Mother and Dad

 If an envelope is missing, the person named in the saluta-tion is given as the addressee. Dates not given in full in the letters have been determined from envelope postmarks and/ or approximated from internal evidence. All information not included in a letter, including the postmark and place of origin on envelopes, is given in brackets. A Census of the letters and enevelopes in the Humanities Research Center Collection is provided at the end of the volume.

AUGUST

1912

I N August 1912, Faulkner's parents and brother Johnsy were away from Oxford briefly. He and his brother Jack (Murry Jr.) stayed that August in the care of their aunt Holland Wilkins, called Auntee, and their grandfather, the Young Colonel, J. W. T. Falkner. Faulkner's letter to his mother, August 16, 1912, is his earliest extant letter.

To Mrs. M. C. Falkner   August 16, 1912
                                 Oxford, Miss.

Dear Miss Lady,

Did you have a good trip? I hope you get some good pictures with my camera. It rained hard yesterday and last night and it is raining now.

They are all good to us, and Lady, Grandfather is the best in the world. I expect he knew that Auntee would be asking to read our letters and so he told Jack and me to come up to the bank that he had plenty of envelopes and paper. This morning at breakfast Jack came in and Big Dad said "Well, heres my old peanut-butter man" and said to me, "Well, Bill, did you sleep good last night?"

Tell Dad that we are looking after the stock all right and tell him if Mr Drew Roane cant get me a lamp Grandfather will buy Beal [Ganongs?] for me. This is an oil lamp but it is a good one. He is letting me try it.

We went to Davidsons bottom in the auto yesterday and what Ches[1] calls 'ar dam' ole leech' got on my foot. He had his head under the skin and Ches cut him out with a butcher knife.

I have seen two little boys that I thought was Johnsy and I was going to town the other day and I saw a man and I started to yell "Hello Dad," when I saw his face. I havent seen any one that looks like you 'cause Lady, you're too pretty.

I'm waiting for a letter.

> Yure erfexxionnite sun
> (Your affectionate son)
> Billie

[1]Ches Caruthers (or Carothers) was J.W.T. Falkner's driver in 1912.

APRIL TO
JUNE

1918

I N the spring of 1918, Faulkner accepted Phil Stone's invitation to join him in New Haven until the end of the academic year at Yale, where Stone was completing his legal studies. His sweetheart Estelle Oldham was engaged to be married that spring to Cornell Franklin, and in part, at least, to get him away from Oxford, Stone arranged a job for Faulkner with a friend at the Winchester Repeating Arms Co. Faulkner arrived in New Haven on April 4 and began work in the accounting office at Winchester on the 10th, for the first time spelling his name "William Faulkner," with a "u." He shared rooms with Stone at 120 York Street, visited at Stone's Corby Court law club, Phi Delta Phi, and met Stone's circle of literary friends who frequented the Brick Row Print and Book Shop at 104 High Street.

He saw airplanes and parades and met British and American military veterans, among them the Canadian recruiting officer Lieutenant Todd, who explained to Faulkner how he might join the Canadian forces as an officer candidate. Faulkner already was writing poetry that had impressed Stone. Now, walking with him in the country or to the seaside on Sunday afternoons, taking a trolley nine miles to Derby to the Yale-Harvard boat races, or watching the Decoration Day parades in New Haven, he was unconsciously gathering and storing the material of fictions he subsequently would write.

By such means, Faulkner's life experiences became the

stuff of his art. But the letters that waken such echoes in the fiction are not self-consciously literary in themselves. Faulkner was twenty years old in the spring of 1918, fascinated with his new surroundings and his urbane new friends, and ready when the opportunity presented itself for another adventure. Early in June, his imagination lighted by the soldiers he saw all about him and by Lieutenant Todd's assurances of quick promotion, he offered himself for service in the British army. Several details of his letters to his mother and father at this time overwhelmingly suggest that he initially intended to enlist not in the R.A.F., which in fact he did, but in the British infantry, expecting to be sent not to Canada, where he went in July, but to England. He went to New York on June 14. On June 15, he resigned his position at the Winchester plant and returned home to Oxford for a brief visit before departing there in July for Toronto.

To Mrs. M.C. Falkner　　　　　Friday [5 April 1918]
[env]　　　　　　　　　　　　[New Haven]

Dear Lady

I am here safely and am about to freeze. I had no idea there would be so much difference in the temperature of Mississippi and Connecticut. There was ice this morning. I wanted to write last night, but it was so cold that Phil and I went straight to bed—there was no heat on last night for some reason.

All Wednesday I rode through the Blue Ridge mountains in Virginia, which is the loveliest country I have ever seen. The fruit trees are in blossom and they looked as though myriads of white and coral butterflies were resting upon them, and the dog wood like bits of silk upon green velvet, and wisps of clouds upon the mountains like flags.

I got to New Haven last night. I am to start work the tenth and I think I shall like it here if it were not for wanting to come home and bother you to death and have you make tea for me and then decide not to drink it. New Haven is about the size of Memphis, but has only two play houses and very few movie places. I went to the Taft, the leading hotel, to have a look at it, this morning. It is not far from my room and from the window I can see three or four Yale men going down the street, with a tin bucket, to get beer at the Taft or the Bishop. And its funny, they all drink, even the faculty members drink with them, but no body ever gets drunk. Every once in a while three or four pass with a tin bucket, then back they come with the pail under an arm, smoking their pipes.

I wish some of the boys at the University of Mississippi could see these men. Tight clothes and pink and yellow shirts are as rare here as negroes, and—outside of the hotel staffs—I have seen one.

I am going out to Winchester this afternoon to look things over.

I'm sorry Jack[1] couldn't have been in New York. I walked down Fifth Avenue to 66th St. and saw the convalescent French and British officers. The lobbies and Mezzanine floors of the hotels are full of them, with their service stripes and wings and game legs and sticks.

In the elevator of the Woodstock yesterday a British aviator was talking to the lift man like this: "I s'y, 'ow munny rawms 'ave 'owve you in this utel?" Translated, how many rooms have you in this hotel?

The man told him and he stared at a point some two inches below my left eye and when the elevator stopped he got out muttering something about a "beastly stupid." I saw a French flyer with only one arm and a Croix de Guerre with two palms, which is about as high as a Frenchman can go and live.

I'm terribly lonesome,

Love
Billy

¹Faulkner's younger brother, Murry C. "Jack" Falkner, Jr.

To Mr. M. C. Falkner   Saturday [6 April 1918]
[env]   [New Haven]

Dear Dad:

I have just come back from Winchester. I am to start work the tenth. The plant is only seven minutes—up here they never say 'Its only about a mile and a half by street car,' they say 'seven minutes'—from our rooms on York Street. They have policemen and plain clothes men all around the plant and there is only one place that the street cars can stop. I suppose I'll be given a badge or a pass word to use. I begin work at eight and have an hour and a half for lunch.

I didnt know there were as big locomotives as I have seen since I came, compounds and double compounds. Through the mountains the road is full of sharp curves and I could look out and see the engine. We lost lots of time. Had to stop at Atkins, Va. and they drew the fires in the engine and put in a new base.

The Southern took us over the first division, Memphis to Bristol, then the Norfolk and Western to Lynchburg, Va, Southern again to Washington; where the Pennsylvania took us to Jersey City and then they gave us an electric engine under the Hudson tubes and into the Penn Station. I am terribly home sick and hope to hear from home by Sunday—tomorrow—anyway Its remarkablye how inexpensively you can live here. My meals cost me only a quarter, unless I want to "blow" myself to something. There are lots of very clean little restaurants here and you can get eggs and toast and coffee at any of them for two bits. So be sure and tell Lady that I shan't starve. There is a newspaper here with a thing like an enormous stock ticker in the window, and as soon as anything happens they show it there, just headlines, of course. This morning it says a British counter-attack has regained the grounds the Germans took yesterday near Amiens. I saw ex-President Taft yesterday.

> Love
> Billy

To Mrs. M. C. Falkner   Saturday [6 April 1918]
[env]   [New Haven]

Darling Momsey

I have so much to tell you that I dont know where to begin. To morrow I'm going to write you everything I know. I went out to Winchester this morning. Get Dad to show you his letter. I have found a place where I can get tea— good tea—and chocolate candy for breakfast every morning.

I love you more than all the world.

> Billy

To Mr. M. C. Falkner   Sunday 8 P.M.
[env]   [7 April 1918]
             [New Haven]

Dear Mother and Dad

Phil and I took a walk this afternoon, out to East Haven and saw the harbor and the ships on the Sound. It was just clear enough to see ~~the~~ Long Island, like a pale blue strip of paint on a sheet of glass. We could see the ships going down to New York and the tiny power- and sail-boats darting about like water bugs. The sea is the most wonderful thing I've seen yet.

We came back about six and had dinner at a Chinese place—paper flowers and butterflies and tea in tiny cups without handles. Phil has been terribly nice to me I can go in a club he belongs to whenever I like.[1]

These people are always saying things to me to hear me talk, though there are lots of Southern people here.

I have met two celebrities. One is a man named Head, who is a poet.[2] Never wears a hat and smokes cigarettes incessantly. He goes around about 40 miles an hour and passes you on the street and never sees you. His clothes look as though he had slept in them and he usually carries about six books with him.

The other is Nicholas Llewellyn[3]. He was in the boche army eight months, at Rheims, and was wounded in the Channel fighting at the first battle of Ypres. He had an iron cross and sent it back when we went to war. He and Lieutenant Todd, a Canadian officer, have some warm arguments as to whether or not the French were using the Rheims cathedral for an artillery observation post.

There are two other English officers here, Captains Massie and Bland. Bland is suffering from shell shock.

The post office is not open Sundays, so I'm hoping to get some letters in the morning.

Give Dean[4] a kiss for brother Bill.

[no signature]

[1]Stone's law club, Phi Delta Phi, located at Corby Court.

[2]Arthur Head, whom Faulkner probably met at the Brick Row Book Shop.

[3]Karl Nickerson Llewellyn taught briefly at the Yale Law School after his graduation before joining the law faculty at Columbia University.

[4] Faulkner's youngest brother, Dean Swift Falkner, sometimes called Sweet.

To Mrs. M. C. Falkner   Tuesday [9 April 1918]
[env]   [New Haven]

Dear Momsey

I had letters you and Dad yesterday, then a wire saying you hadn't heard from me. This is a rotten postal system. I cant understand why you hadn't gotten the letters I wrote Friday morning. I also had two letters this morning, in one envelope.

My trunk hasn't come yet. I hope I shant have to buy any more clothes. Phil has moved some of his things to give me two more drawers in his chiffonier, but if my trunk doesn't come I shant need 'em.

I met a real, dyed-in-the wool Englishman. He is stupidly clever and says "awsk," and "hawf," and "cawn't" and "ither" in place of "either." Name's Reed.[1]

I'm having a great time now. I dont have to get up until eleven o'clock, thereby saving one meal. I start work in the morning, however. I like my boss. his name's Cook.

Love to Dad & the boys

[no signature]

[1]Bernard Reed, who later in the spring wrote Faulkner a character reference for the R.A.F.

To Mrs. M. C. Falkner Sunday [14 April 1918]
[env] [New Haven]

I have become a full fledged working man now, I know just what I have to do, have my badge and am getting twenty dollars a week

Yesterday I went through the plant and saw the rifle and machine gun assembling rooms. They are making Browning guns. There are eighteen thousand people working there, probably half of them are women and girls, in the machine shops even. I work only eight hours a day and have Saturday afternoon off.

I am cold all the time. Woke up yesterday with snow on the ground. My trunk has not come yet. You certainly saved my life with the shirt which came yesterday. Saved me buying one. I have my laundry now, so I'm all right.

New Haven is a wonderful old place. The streets have names like George, Crown, College, Chapel, Orange. Phil and I are living at 120 York street. There are two men living here, a Mr. Smith[1] and Mr Noon—he's Irish. They have been very nice to me. Ray Noon just wandered in and said— "Give her my love, Bill"—taking it that I was writing to a flapper. I told him it it was you, and he said—"Then be sure and send my message, and tell her we have only had to get you out of jail twice." He is tutor or travelling companion to a 17 year old kid who is heir to two fortunes. They go every where. Took Phil and me with them to Meriden to-day in a car. Give Dad my love and tell him I have seen one of the largest hardware houses in America.

Billy

[1]S. B. "Smitty" Smith, who was a principal in the New Haven City Schools.

To Mrs. M. C. Falkner   Sunday [21 April 1918]
[env]   [New Haven]

I am having a good time. All these people are awfully nice to me. I never had as much fun in my life as I did yesterday. Phil and Lieutenant Todd, the Canadian, went to a La Crosse game between Yale and Stevens. La Cross is indigent [sic] with the Indians and is played with a hard rubber ball and every man has a bat something on the order of a monstrous snow-shoe and the game seems to be a cross between "skinny" and first degree murder. And funny! You would have died watching ~~each other~~ them bat each other about.

The Yale goal-keeper had a costume something like that of a deep sea diver, and when ever they play came near him, he would yell—

"Kill that man! Kill that man and take that ball away from him!"

Then you'd see a man tearing down the field with the ball in his "Crosse" like a rock in a butter fly net, with an opposing player holding him by the arm or the jersey, his bat upraised in his right hand as though he were saying, or hissing, rather:

"Drop it! Drop it! or I'll knock your damned head off!" I laughed until I was weak.

Last night I went to a party at Corby Court, Phil's law club. The German soldier (ex) and a man from California named Starr,[1] and I took four quart milk bottles and went over to the Bishop Hotel and got some beer. Then we sat around and smoked pipes and talked and the Boche sang us some German drinking songs.

I like my work very well. There are Harvard and Yale and Penn. men working out there. I was late Saturday for the first time. Phil set the alarm for 8 instead of seven, so when I got there I fooled them and went up and told Mr Cook how and why I was late, and he just "laffed," and I'm all right. I think he liked it.

These people up here eat more pie and doughnuts for breakfast. You never have any hot bread up here, so when they start telling me what a fine place the East is, I tell them what hot biscuits and waffles are like. They have quite a lot of respect for Southerners up here.

Golly, I wish I could wake up at home in the morning.

Billy

Tell me about Estelle's wedding.[2]

[1]Stone's friend and fellow law student Hubert Starr.
[2]Estelle Oldham married Cornell Franklin in Oxford, April 18, 1918.

To Mr. and Mrs. M. C.
Falkner   Wednesday [24 April 1918]
                             [New Haven]

Dear Mother and Dad:

I have just left a bridge game to write this. We play nearly every night. There is a real Englishman who comes over to play with us. He is very nice—says "thuht-een" and "bean" in place of "been." His names Reed—Bernard Reed.

Working up here is agreeing with me. I am eating more than I ever ate in my life, I think, lots of meat. They eat lots of pie up here and I have acquired the pie habit. I think I have gained some. So if you ever run out of things to send me, send grub. I haven't had any thing except machine—or Union—made vits since I came.

It has turned warm, thank heaven. But my trunk has not come yet. They are tracing it for me.

I get my first pay to-morrow. They make you work two weeks before they pay you at all—I mean, I will be paid for two weeks at one time. It will be just my luck to have the whole damned plant blow up to-morrow at noon, when I cant watch things.

I made another tour of inspection to-day, and as I had no pass, it was undeniably piquant. I saw them making the H.E. shells—five and six point ones, about a yard long.

This is an awfully nice badge I have. I wish I could send it to Sweet. It looks like this: [FIGURE]¹ I have to punch a time clock every time I go in and come out.

There was a plane over from Long Island today. It looked so short and small that I think it was French. It flipped and darted about a while, rolled over and dived and then went back.

There are lots of Britishers here, in their caps and belts and plain, straight khaki trousers. No leggings or boots at all.

Phil is going to mail this for me now.

Love,
Billy

P.S. Dad, I got your letter today. Thank you, sir, and I love you.

Bill

Momsey: I couldn't live here at all but for your letters. I love you darling. Good boy!

---

¹Line drawing of the Winchester badge inscribed "2A1/AGB Office/1680."

To Mrs. M. C. Falkner   Sunday [28 April 1918]
[New Haven]

Darling Momsey

I hope you have your flowers by now. Phil and I had the man telegraph and send them out from Memphis. We had two red carnations, Phil and I, to wear to-day. Nearly every one—excepting the impossibles—had them on to-day, thought was rather cold and bad out.

At the Oneco hotel tonight there was a wounded British "Tommy" with a Distinguished Conduct Medal and a stiff leg. He looked American, perhaps was, but had evidently been in the "show." It's funny to walk the streets and look at these people—Poles, Russians, Italian Communists, all with American flags in their lapels. And yet they say that God made man in his own image. [FIGURE][1]

There was a French official War film here, but I didn't know it until to late to go.

I saw Martha Hedman in "The Boomerang" last night. Weve seen her in the movies at home, if you remember.

Phil and I walked out to East Rock yesterday afternoon. it is about 200 feet high and from the top you can see all the way across New Haven to the ocean, and tiny lighthouses as stiff and white as pieces of chalk, and a Sound steamer like a toy ship on a mirror, came up and docked. The day was so clear we could see the houses on Long Island and little sail boats like wisps of smoke and the water was the bluest blue I ever saw.

I have broken into poetry again. Phil has sent it to a magazine and I am sending you a copy. As regards sending me clothes—shirts—shirts—shirts. And please, Mother dear, make them with *one* button instead of two at the collar—not - [FIGURE] but [FIGURE]² so the collar will be lower. The laundry men here have a nasty habit of ironing them off, so these will be lest repairing for me to do.

Tell Dean to write and tell me how his candy went and give Sallie³ my love when you see her

Love more than all the world.
[no signature]

¹Line drawing of a heavily mustached man with a flag in his lapel.
²Sketches of two- and one-button shirt collars.
³Faulkner's cousin, Sallie Murry Wilkins.

To Mrs. M. C. Falkner   [postmarked 5 May 1918]
[env]   [New Haven]

Dear Mother:

I say to let Jack go by all means.¹ He is doing nothing there, will continue to if you keep him there. I know how he feels about it. Some times I used to feel that if I didn't get to go that I could never forgive you for not letting me go and drive an ambulance when I wanted to so much. If he goes in the Q.M. Corps he can make something of him self, when as it is now, he'll keep on until they catch him playing cards, or a similar brand of assininity. He can get things there now that he'll not be able to later.

I wish you could see these people. Every family has some one over there, and you can pick their faces out of any crowd in the world.

I went for a walk this afternoon and I am terribly tired. Did Dean get the candy I sent? Tell Mammy² that I have

lunch every day with two niggers. They are Hindoos, but
dont tell her that.

My trunk hasn't come yet.

[no signature]

---

[1] Jack Falkner enlisted in the Marine Corps in May 1918 and trained at Parris Island,
South Carolina, and Quantico, Virginia.
[2] Falkner family servant Mammy Caroline Barr (1840–1940).

To Mrs. M. C. Falkner   Sunday [19 May 1918]
[env]   [New Haven]

I cant realize that big, selfish objective Ed Beanland is
dead. It's like hearing that a lightning rod has been struck
by lightning. I suppose his people are taking it rather hard.
I am going to get Dean, poor kid, some more candy to
morrow and send it. Dont tell him though; for it may not
reach him either. There is evidently some postal clerk between ̶h̶ us with an awful sweet tooth. Of course I sealed up
the other letter without my two poems, which I am sending
this time. I rather like the shorter one. Show them to Katrina[1] when you see her. I just had dinner with two British
officers, Lieutenant Todd, who was wounded at Vimy Ridge
last year, and a tall, taciturn Scotchman named MacIntosh.
The evening papers are full of the death of Major Raoul
Lufbery, the New Haven aviator in the Lafayette Escadrille.[2] So there's only one of them left now, Captain William
Thaw. Dont you know he's lonesome! All six of them were
Yale men; enlisted in the French Foreign Legion in '14,
then were transferred to the Flying Corps. First it was
Kiffen Rockwell, then Norman Prince, then Victor Chap-

man was shot down over Le Caleau as he was carrying some oranges to Prince in the hospital, then Bert Hall about two weeks ago, and now its Lufbery. His picture is in a photographer's window on Chapel Street. I imagine Thaw feels that he's been left holding the sack.

I am holding three jobs now. One of them keeps me chasing all over the plant. I am seriously considering that they furnish me with roller skates. Spring has at last arrived—I am wearing my white "pants" and I fel feel natural again. We went to Momauguin, a resort at the sea. It was wonderful. I wish you could see it—the indescribable blue of the sea and the sky, and tiny white sails on the water and tiny white clouds, like their reflections in the sky, ambling along as gravely and demurely as very clean little girls on Sunday mornings. And canoes—one with the o sub aquatic propensiter of a U-boat—and Irish girls and teeth and chewing gum and the filthy, sturdy, unkillable infants of the very poor—verily, they shall inherit the earth—and the rustling of the sea like a ball room full of ladies in silken dresses. We lay on the sand and my hair is becoming sunburned on top again and didn't think and had a wonderful. There were people in bathing—washing?—but I couldn't see it, as it was rather cool. The other morning, Phil came in to wake me, and I said—Go away and let me alone, Mother, dont you know this is a heatless day?

It certainly is hard to get up in the morning. They pull me out and hang my clothes one me and off we go to breakfast—I in a semi-stupified condition. I never know whether I eat breakfast or not, but you should see me eat at night. I'll eat my self out of house and home yet. Give Dean this gum, but dont tell him about his candy, just so he'll not be disappointed twice. I'm afraid from your last letter that he didn't get either of the boxes I sent him. I got your cake and jelly

and wrote you the next day thanking you for them. I am
now gunning for my trunk.

Love
Billy

¹Faulkner and Stone's Oxford friend Katrina Carter.

²Faulkner is confused about the facts of Lufbery's and his companions' service.
Major Raoul Lufbery was from Wallingford, Connecticutt, not New Haven. Kiffen
Rockwell, Bert Hall, Norman Prince, Victor Chapman, and William Thaw were members of the original Lafayette Escadrille formed in April 1916. Only Thaw had been a
student at Yale. Lufbery joined them in May 1916, and prior to his death on May 19,
1918, achieved the status of American "ace of aces." Victor Chapman died on June 23,
1916, shot down taking oranges to Clyde Balsey, not to Prince. Prince was shot down
and died on October 15, 1916. Kiffin Rockwell died on September 23, 1916. Thaw and
Bert Hall survived the war: Faulkner may have confused Hall with another Lafayette
Escadrille pilot, James N. "Jimmy" Hall, who was taken prisoner by the Germans on
May 17, 1918.

To Mrs. M. C. Falkner   [postmarked 27 May 1918]
[env]   [New Haven]

I went out to the Light House with Smitty this afternoon,
and ate ice cream cones and did *not* go to the ball game they
had. The Yale-Harvard boat race is going to be here next
Saturday, on the Housatonic River. They have an observation train which follows the race along the shore. I shan't
miss that.

I am seriously thinking of coming home with Phil about
July 1st, provided I have any money—for the bill has gone
through drafting me when I become of age and as I had
much rather beat them to it and enlist, I'd like to be home
about a month before hand. I am going down to the station
to morrow and tell them that I'll have my trunk or the
money in one week.

It certainly will be good to be at home again, if I can come.

Love
Billy

To Mrs. M. C. Falkner   [30 May 1918]
[New Haven]

My dear lady—

This was Liberty Bond day here,¹ and there were parades on every street and alley—blind ones included. Speaking of blind alleys, as we were coming out of the Oneco hotel— dinner—tonight, an aged inebriate came out ahead of us, or rather, he stood at the door until we came and opened it for it him. He looked exactly like old my Mr. Meek. He was standing at the bar as we came through the first time. He handed the bar-man a two dollar bill. I suppose the bar man let him drink two dollars worth and then sent him out. And from the edge he had on, I should say the bar-man short changed him self.

But back to the parades. The Yale army and navy Corps were out in force with bands and banners, the tank was banging away.

A plane came over from the flying school at Marlin, and stayed over New Haven three hours, dropping propaganda and one $50.00 Bond. It came back just before it left and, just over the green, stood perfectly motionless on its tail for several seconds at about two thousand feet; then dived nose first, looped three times and finished about three hundred feet up, lying on its back.

And we could see the pilots face, pink as a peach blossom, as though we were looking down on him. Before he left, another came and they had a mimic battle, dipping and darting at each other, so low we could see the smoke from the exhausts. There was a man climbed the face of the Woolworth building this afternoon—here—, with a liberty Bond on his back.

I am looking forward to the cake. I have written Dean one. I hope he can read it himself. Make him try, though.

The sub-office manager of my office saw some of my writing the other day and he asked me if I could print. I told him I fancied one could acquire that power, as it is nothing to make a dust about. Then he said—Perhaps you'd better try it.

And perhaps I shall. You can never tell, however.

I saw one of the most attractive girls this afternoon. She sells cheap jewelry at Woolworth's. I bought a gaudy comb which I am sending Mammy, to talk to her. When she found I was from the South, we became great friends. She has pale gold hair and her eyes were so blue they are almost black, and she has slim hands—thank heaven. I wish you could see her. She isn't small, but she is as exquisite as a Dresden vase, or a figure by Tanagra.

She is wonderfully lovely. Sounds as though I were raving, but I am not. I really would like to have her where I could sit and look at her when ever I liked.

I heard a story of a certain member of the Quartermasters Corps at a Texas camp, who was transferred to the Engineers Corps, and the Quartermasters Corp's hung out a service flag.

I Love you,
Billy

[1]Liberty Bond Day was observed in New Haven in 1918 on Decoration Day, May 30.

To Mrs. M. C. Falkner   Sunday [2 June 1918]
[env]   [New Haven]

Dear Mother:

I've been having a strenuous week of it. There was a
holiday Thursday. I got up at ten o'clock and had to dodge
three parades to get to breakfast. This is the darndest town
for parades and perambulaters I have ever seen. Yesterday
afternoon Phil and I went to the Yale-Harvard ball game.
Yale won, though I dont know the score, not being especially keen on ball games; then we rode on the trolley nine
miles to Derby and saw the boat race. It took us three hours
to get back. Never had such an uncomfortable trip in my
life. It was worth it, however, for the race was wonderful.
We were on a high bluff over the Housatonic River. It was
about seven o'clock and everything was wonderfully still, so
still that we could hear the band across the river playing,
and the river was dotted with canoes and bits of color, reflections from the girls' dresses on the other side. We could
see the shells about a half mile off, with the judge's boat—
starters boat—just behind them. Harvard won aby a boat's
length. You should have seen the crew go out, one man fell
backward in the Yale boat, just like he'd been shot, and one
man dived overboard. It certainly must take every thing out
of them. Then we could hear Harvard cheer, and say "Hah-
vud, Hah-vud."

At the ball game every one stood up during Yales half of
the seventh inning, and sang "Goodnight, poor Harvard,"
while the band played. I wish Dean could have seen the
cheer leaders.

And if Mammy could have seen that Decoration Day parade. The colored troops were there, veterans of the civil
war, dolled up in blue suits and cigars and medals until they
all looked like brigadiers.

When the veterans passed, a ~~man~~ fellow named DeLacey[1]
who was watching the parade said to me—"Well, Bill, you
ought to salute the old ~~boys~~ boys. It was your grandfather
and his friends that put him that way." I told him that I
thought they should salute me, for had it not been for my
grandfather and his friends they would ~~b~~ not have had any
war to go to. Even the Italians had a parade, including one
nigger with an Italian flag and a cigar. They were certainly
funny. They all were short and fierce like brigands. The
Chinese, for some reason, didn't have one.

My trunk came finally. Tell Dad that I am going to look
into that matter as soon as the bank opens in the morning—
His letter came last night, and then I will write him tomorrow night.

I went out to double beach this afternoon and had my
first swim in the ocean. I dont see how any one ever drowns
in the sea. You can float like a cigar box. And I was surprised to see how few people here can really swim, to have
all this water to practise in.

I was in a drug store the other day, having some ice
cream, and I suggested a change to the clerk. He complied,
and said, "Makes it better, doesn't it?" And without thinking, I said "It sho' God does," and a fellow, about 21 or so,
whirled about to me and said, "My God, are you from the
South, too?" He was from Georgia.

Love
Billy

---

[1] Al DeLacey, a friend of Stone's who worked in the Brick Row Book Shop.

To Mrs. M. C. Falkner   [postmarked 7 June 1918]
[env]   [New Haven]

Darling Momsey: and Dad
  I have got an chance to join up with the British and get a
commission as second lieutenant—leftenant they call it—in
about three months after I am sent to training camp. It's a
wonderful chance, for there is no thing to be had in the U.S.
Army now, except a good job stopping boche bullets as a
private. I have got to know Lieutenant Todd rather well,
and he's explained things to me. The English are trying to
get officers now—they have two million unofficial reserve
troops in house now, which they cant use at all. I can enlist
as a second year Yale man, he will recommend me for a
commission at once. It's the chance I've been waiting for
now. Every thing will be my way, I can almost have my pick
of anything, I'll be in at the wind up of the show. The
chances of advancement in the English Army are very good;
I'll perhaps be a major at the end of a year's service. I've
thought about it constantly. This chance will not last, as
Todd is going next week and then it will be a bit harder, I
shall probably have to enlist in the line and take my chances
of promotion, which I'd rather do than get in the U.S. Army
and be sent into action under an inexperienced officer. The
English officers are the best yet, take better care of their
men and weigh all chances for them. So I shall learn war in
the best of schools, where the elimination of risk is taught
above every thing. So I think I shall enlist to-morrow. Then
I shall be given a month's furlough before sailing for England.
  Its rather hard to explain in a letter just how I feel, but
you both know that already, how badly I've always desired
to go. At the rate I am living now, I'll never be able to make

anything of myself, but with this business I will be fixed up after the war is over.

Love
Billy

To Mrs. M. C. Falkner   Thursday 8 P.M.
[env]   [13 June 1918]
                               [New Haven]

Dearest Mother

I have just received your letter and when I try to tell you how good it has made me feel I become entangled in a thicket of verbiage. I am going to do that as soon as I get home.

I go down to New York tomorrow to see Lieutenant-Colonel Lord Wellesley,[1] to straighten out details and fix up my furlough, and I think I shall start home with Phil Saturday night. Of this I cant be sure. I will find out from Lord Wellesley where I am to be trained and when I sail for England. The big schools are at Oxford and Cambridge. It will be wonderful just seeing England and those places. Lieutenant Todd has been very nice to me, telling me ~~so~~ not to address Colonel Wellesley as "yer ludship" or "me lud," simply as "sir." I have three letters—one from a high school principal, one from the doctor of ancient literature in Yale, and one from a native Englishman.[2] I have some money, enough to come back on, but I'll have to draw on Dad for part of my fare home. That was a wonderful letter of yours. I showed it to Phil and he said "Isnt she wonderful, God Bless her," and I went him one better and told him that anyone who wrote letters like that and cared for me as you evidently do, didn't need God's blessing. You are an angel,

Mother darling. I'll wire when I am leaving New York. I am too enthusiastic to write any more now.

                                                        Love
                                                        Billy

[1]Lord Wellesley was officer in charge of the Royal Air Force Cadet Recruiting Office at 220 West 42nd Street in New York.

[2]Probably the principal was S. B. "Smitty" Smith and the Englishman Bernard Reed, both of whom had rooms with Faulkner at 120 York Street in New Haven.

JULY TO
DECEMBER

1918

WILLIAM Faulkner, spelled with a "u," enlisted in the Royal Air Force in New York in June 1918. After a three-week pre-induction furlough in Oxford, he returned to New York on July 8 and was sent on from there to Toronto for formal induction. There he successfully passed a battery of tests and was accepted in Class "A" as Cadet-for-Pilot. He was issued an ill-fitting uniform, and assigned to temporary duty at the Recruits' Depot at the Jesse Ketchum School barracks. He was there for three weeks before moving to the basic training camp at Long Branch, on the shore of Lake Ontario west of Toronto. By the time his mail caught up with him at the end of his second week in Canada, he had written nine letters home and sent a wire.

His letter-writing was not a matter of homesickness. Instead, he was eager to tell his family about his adventure in the north, to recount his successes and to express his hopes for the immediate future. As a group, the sixty-three letters and telegrams from Canada show him to have been a serious and enthusiastic cadet-pilot whose soldierly cynicism about the military institution never overcame his reverence for the World War I heroes of the trenches and the sky nor blunted his own optimistic expectations of joining "the show" himself. In that reverence and those expectations, however, there lay the seeds of self-invention.

In April 1918, two months prior to his enlistment, the Royal Flying Corps of Faulkner's romantic imaginings was

renamed the Royal Air Force; in November the Armistice
found him one week short of completing ground school. He
was demobilized early in December, almost certainly without having flown, and discharged in January "in conse-
quence of being Surplus to R.A.F. requirements." For
Faulkner, however, the romance of the Royal Flying Corps
and of flight never dissipated. If he was not an officer in fact,
he saw himself as a dutiful trainee who had learned "all the
dope that officers have to know." He was pleased to be
mistaken in Toronto once for "a flying officer in mufti," and
when he bought a pilot's brevet pin as a gift for his mother,
he bought one for himself as well, and an officer's overcoat,
he reported, without mentioning that he also had purchased
the rest of the uniform. "I have so much to tell," he promised his mother, "things that I was not allowed to write
about while the war was on," and he added, as if to justify
his failure to write in detail on this subject, "in fact, we were
not allowed to say anything at all about flying."

At the end, waiting restlessly for demobilization, he was
torn between his disappointed hopes and his longing for
home. There were inconsistencies now from one to another
of his letters, but he seems not to have noticed. Or cared. In
fact, he seems to have used his letters to document what
R.A.F. records do not. In November he congratulated himself on having four hours of solo flying, then expressed his
disappointment that the "Royal Flying Corps" would not
give him the one more hour that would make him eligible
for a civilian pilot's certificate and membership in the International Aero Club. Twice during this time he wrote that
there would be no more flying in Canada, but between times
he claimed to have flown. "I came down the other day," he
said, "so cold that I had to be lifted out of the machine." In
the years immediately following his Canadian campaign, the
guises and disguises of his letters from Canada also would

become the stuff of his fiction, and his stories of military heroism would find their way into biographical notes about him. In truth, as he would say of a fictional character from his first novel, and as these letters verify, Cadet William Faulkner was one for whom the war had ended too soon.

To Mrs. M. C. Falkner   Monday 10 AM
[env]   [8 July 1918]
                                            [New York]

We are just approaching Philadelphia. The sea along here from Baltimore is wonderful—such colors you never saw. They played a trick on us this morning, left us at Washington by mistake, consequently we are six hours late. I certainly have been nasty and dirty. This morning, however, I shaved and washed my head—all of it—and I am a bit more respectable. I hope I shant shock Captain Sise too badly.

If possible I shall find from them an address and you can write me.

I certainly aver missing my "vits." They do one very poorly on these blooming trains in the States, and then the blighters want one's gold tooth for it.

                                   I love you
                                   Billy

Love to Dad and tell him I shall write as soon as I become settled.

To Mrs. M. C. Falkner   July 8, 1918
[telegram]   2:30 PM
                                      New York,
                                      NY

ULTIMATELY ARRIVED DID I LOVE TO DAD AND DEAN

[t]WILLIAM FALKNER

To Mrs. M. C. Falkner   July 8 12 PM [1918]
[postcard]   [Albany, NY]

Ever since we left New York weve been going along the
Hudson river. The sun on the palisades is wonderful, and
West Point like a grim medieval fortress glowering at us.
Carrying on, sure enough now. Toronto in the morning. I
shall write to-morrow and tell you in detail how I came out
at the R.C.F.R.M. in New York. Another Cadet and I are
making the trip together. Wish you were here.

                                      Billy

To Mrs. M. C. Faulkner   Tuesday [9 July 1918]
[env]   Toronto

Mother darling—

This certainly is an English place—London "Bobbies"
with their capes and high conical hats and no one here is in a
hurry as are cities in the states. These people are wonderful
to me. There was a Canadian—who has seen three years of
war— at the station to meet incipient aviators, the porters
and bell boys dont take tips from us. This is a place full of
short crooked streets and old houses, and soldiers everywhere—Canadian infantry men some who seem to be forty

years old with bushy mustaches. No wonder the Huns dont like them. We passed the flying camp on the train this morning. It is Longbranch, on Lake Ontario, which looks like the sea, excepting you can see the United States across it.

Yesterday, when I got my passport and transportation from Lieut. Col. Lord Wellesley, he said—If There are two kinds of pilots—officer-pilots and sergeant-pilots, and if you faint in the revolving chair test, you will be made a gunner-observer in stead of pilot. Do you agree to go under these conditions? I said—Yes—taking off one who is really keen, you know—and so he put me in Class "A."

I didn't know what this meant, so I asked the sergeant. He tells me that it means that I am recommended by Lord Wellesley, who is commander-in-chief of the Royal Air Force,[1] for a commission as lieutenant-pilot. So all I must do is to keep from fainting in the chair test. I have no intention of fainting, however.

Lieutenant Todd, the New Havener, is coming up Wednesday night to go into training, so we shall be trained together, if I come through.

I am sending you and Dad flags. The Canadian service flag has a maple leaf in it—a live leaf, and when it begins to turn crimson it is very pretty.

I love you
Billy

I'll find my address to night and write you a card.

[1]Faulkner is exaggerating. Lord Wellesley was in command of the R.A.F. Cadet Recruiting Office in New York.

To Mrs. M. C. Faulkner   [postmarked 9 July 1918]
[env]   [Toronto]

Dear Mother and Dad

I passed my examination today and I would not go through with what I have today for all the democracy that could be produced. It was about ten times as bad as the one in New York. I've been at it all day. From 10 to 6—union hours. They went all over me again and this afternoon at 5 I got the chair. My being a pilot or a gunner-observer depended on this, for Col. Wellesley had recommended me for a commission.

They put me in the chair and had me focus my eyes on a bulls eye about 15 yards off, I closed my eyes and they whirled me by machinery. Then ~~whe~~ I had to focus on the bulls-eye again, which had failed to stop when I did, and they timed me to see how long it took me to re-focus. Then they whirled me the other way. Same thing. Next they whirled me so fast that I had to hold in, stopped me and put my finger—eyes still closed—on a mark, made me move it and replace it. Of course, I felt as though I were still whirling. Then I had to lean forward with my head touching me knees. This gave the sensation of the chair revolving at a 45 degree angle. Stopped me, then the other direction.

They kept this up for about 30 minutes and I was beginning to fear that I wouldn't faint, being terribly sick, when the doctor said—all right. You can dress now.

There were three poor devils who failed on the chair test, so I was the only pilot to qualify. Three observers did, however. They are not given the chair test. I am still groggy from it, but the next time I get to see you I shall be a lieutenant-pilot. I am to be "sent up" to morrow at 10:30, and then I shall have an address. At present I am at the King Edward "Uhtel" having arrived here with ten dollars. Lord

Wellesley recommended that I go here. Evidently thinks I'm a blinkin' lord myself.

Shall send my picture as soon as I get my uniform.

Love,
Billy

To Mrs. M. C. Faulkner [postmarked 10 July 1918]
[env] [Toronto]

I've just passed another day of examinations and reexaminations and have been left in Class "A." A commission if I stick, and to night at 9:30 I go to the barracks and then I'll have an address. I certainly am tired and I know these next three weeks will be hard going. Know I shant like it—a board and a blanket to sleep on, and so forth. However, if it takes this to become a flyer, I'm willing.

I shall go to work to-morrow, so whenever my letters miss a day, dont worry, just take consolation in the fact that for once I am truly working. I do wish I could play Rip Van Winkle for about 3 weeks though. I get a Cadet's uniform tomorrow, and I'll have my picture taken.

I certainly miss my vits at home. However! Give Katrina my love and tell her I'll write when I get time. Grand father also. This penny is Deans.

Love
Billy

To Mrs. M. C. Faulkner   Thursday [11 July 1918]
[env]   [Toronto]

I have an address now—

     Cadet William Faulkner
     Reg No 173799
     Royal Air Force
     Jessie Ketcham School
     Toronto, Ontario, Canada

The barracks is a high school building where we shall be perhaps six weeks, unless we are sent to Hamilton, Ontario, for some training To morrow we get rookie uniforms and begin training—mopping floors and such, so when I get through I'll more than likely make some one a nice wife.

More examinations to-day, which makes about 4 days of it. I slept—or rather, did not sleep—on a board last night— my bunk.

The food is not so bad. Perhaps when I get to work I'll become hungry and really enjoy it. We were measured for our officer's uniforms today, to get provided we stick in class A. As a cadet, I rank a sergeant and am just under a lieutenant I make my own bed, blankets must be folded the same way, and wash my own dishes. Its a fine life—if you dont care especially what you say. I'm not grumbling, how- ever.

               Billy

To Mrs. M. C. Faulkner Saturday [13 July 1918]
[env] [Toronto]

Mother darling

I've been at it for 24 hours now. We got our uniforms yesterday morning[1]—a tiny cap with a white band, a double breasted tunic with Royal Flying Corp on each shoulder, enormous boots and spiral putties and a stick to keep our hands out of our pockets—had were inspected by an officer, and were put on fire picket at 4:50. Three of us, however, were picked from the flock and set as pickets to Crawford St. barracks. We were there 24 hours, were guards two hours and slept four, guards two more, and so on, challenging every man who entered. I thought we had caught the bad luck, until I came back and found the others had been down town all day cleaning the Royal Air Force building.

I have a complete outfit now, and must send all my other stuff home. I'll write you the day I send it, so you can look out for it.

They made us get out on the streets today to learn how to salute. The British are great sticklers for this and it must be done right.

The drill corporals and sergeants here are all English— drop their h's and say 'blinkin' ' and 'bloody' on all occasions. And give us hell.

To morrow we have church parade—fancy my going to church. The British army is going to reform me after all.

We can see planes from the aviation field in the air all the time.

Love
Billy

[1]R.A.F. cadets in Canada in 1918 were issued old Royal Flying Corps air mechanic's uniforms complete with R.F.C. shoulder tabs.

To Mrs. M. C. Faulkner   Monday 10:30 A.M.
[env]   [15 July 1918]
                                 [Toronto]

Dear Mother

I am having rifle drill this morning. On parade the officer found a hook undone on my tunic. Wish I were not so careless that way, or there were not so many buttons on my tunic.

Had nine hours leave from noon yesterday and went with another cadet and an infantry Captain we know to a resort. It was funny to see the other cadets look at us—running about with officers. There are lots of American soldiers here and a few French. I'm certainly living fast—up at six, work all day, and in bed at 10:15. Awful food, however. I had one good meal last night at the King Edward Hotel with the captain.

They move the Cadets in and out of this barracks so much that we are the old fellows now.

We are preparing for barracks inspection this morning. Corporals and orderlies running about and tearing down things and making us put them back again. It's a great life. I dont even have time to read. Learning the Morse code in my spare moments we are required to be able to send and receive six words a minute.

Give my love to Dean and Dad. I am expecting to be able to hear from home by Thursday.

                                             Billy

          Cadet William Faulkner
          Reg. No. 173799
          Royal Air Force
          Toronto Jessie Ketcham School

To Mrs. M. C. Faulkner   Tuesday [16 July 1918]
[env]   [Toronto]

Dear Mother

I got your wire today, and one from Phil also. Still at it and I'm beginning to eat more now. We have a complete kit, summer outfit also, and they make us shave every morning. Heres the way I look now—trunks and a cork helmet, like a polo helmet, and the eternal stick [FIGURE].[1] We cant leave barracks without it. Been having rifle drill yesterday and today. The drill corporal is an English "Tommy" who was at Mons in 1915, and Armentieres. sent home discharged for shell shock, and then enlisted in the Flying Corps as a mechanic. He said that he and two other men were in listening post in a sap, when the huns blew them up. He doesnt remember where, nor when it was. He showed us how to bayonet and shoot the body away. His name is 'Arry something and he carries his cigarettes behind his ears. I was on picket last night from twelve to three and didnt have to get up until nine today.

I certainly was glad to get the wire, for I wasnt expecting to hear before Thursday. I wish you could see some of these flight sergeants and mechanics—fierce mustaches and waists like corset models and tiny caps and swagger sticks.

They require us to buy a pair of nice shoes for walking out—when we are given our uniform—the new ones—and a cane with a silver handle. Very foolish and very British, however. I am quite proficient in telegraphy now. I shall pass that test, I think. If we pass 75% of our work, we are lieutenants, 50%, sergeant pilots, below that, mechanics. I am hoping to be moved to Long Branch soon and I am going to try to get one of the cadets to let me make a flight with him out at Lake Side.

Love
Billy

---

[1]Line drawing of a soldier in summer uniform of pith helmet, short-sleeved shirt, short pants, and knee socks.

To Mrs. M. C. Faulkner   Friday [19 July 1918]
[env]   [Toronto]

Dear Mother and Dad

I got five letters yesterday, first I've gotten, five in a bunch, think of it. I've had several things happen to me today, so I have time now to really write. First was, on parade this morning they pulled me up because I completely forgot to shave, and I was to have had 3 extra parades for it. So I beat it up to the M.O. and was inoculated, so I dont have to parade, and then they made me room orderly, which means I lie in my bunk and see that two poor fellows scrub the floor properly. So I've nothing to do until tomorrow.

They certainly have attractive weather here, its just cool enough to wear a light sweater, and terribly clear. Every where I look I see planes from the flying schools. This is a great fruit growing country, orchards every where. Every thing here is much cheaper.   last night I had leave until Mid night and down town I got some pork, mashed potatoes, macaroni au gratin and peaches and cream and tea for 75¢. This place is about twice as big as Memphis. Some wonderful homes here. The streets are wide and there is no hurry. They have very English signs here—Nichols, Ni-

chols and Nichols; Barristers, they never say lawyer. I went
last night and heard Sousa's band. The streets here are full
of soldiers and I am kept saluting all the time. They are very
strict about this. We must value the uniform. There are
wounded of all descriptions here—Scotch in kilts, French,
Canadians, English.

My inoculation didnt hurt at all. My shoulder smarts just
a bit, and is getting stiff. They make me keep swinging it. Its
funny, but I have read absolutely no war news since I came,
dont know what barn yards have been captured and lost.
People up here are too close to it to read news papers. They
are sending bunches of flyers over seas constantly from here

The barracks is a distributing depot. All new men and
graduated men come here. I'll certainly be glad when I
come back here as an officer. It seems that I shall never get
down town in the day so I can have a picture made to send
you.

Next time you write Jack send him my address and ask
him to write if he is not as busy as I am, but if he is, tell him
not to bother, and make John write me. Tell Dean I got his
letter, bless his heart, and I shall send him something when
I can.

Give Grandfather my love, and Sallie and Auntee.[1]

Billy

---

[1]Faulkner's cousin, Sallie Murry Wilkins, and her mother, Mary Holland Falkner
Wilkins.

To Mrs. M. C. Faulkner   Monday 5:30
[env]   [22 July
                                            1918]
                                            [Toronto]

Dear Mother—

Ive been on another 24 hour picket—at Crawford st. 2
hours on an four hours off. Needless to say, I didnt sleep
much. The post office is open, and I am going down when I
finish this to see if I have some more mail. I got a bunch
Thursday and I hope I have some today.

Its turned suddenly warm, and on this picket they made
us wear our winter clothes   It was awful. I cant seem to get
down town before six o'clock to get my picture made to
send you. This is a queer army. We will be paid in two
weeks, in the mean time we must buy a kit bag, dress putties, and dress shoes, so I am afraid I shall need $10. I cant
tell yet, however. But shall write if things become crucial.

We are expecting to be moved to Long Branch Saturday.
Its another hardening process place.

We got in too late for supper—its tea, really, at 4, bread
and butter and "plum and apple" jam, and tea. So we didnt
get any. Therefore, I'm going down to squander 35¢ on food
and a taxi-cab driver's place where they do one very well.

We have the conventional army stuff. Bully beef, plum
and apple jam—the tins of th from which they make wells
bombs. I think they would be as deadly as we get them here
as they would be filled with T.N.T.

I am going to write Grandfather tomorrow.

                                        I love you
                                        Billy

To Mrs. M. C. Faulkner   Tuesday [23 July 1918]
[env]   [Toronto]

I got your letter yesterday. Tell Jack that he's lucky if he gets salmon for his tea. Mondays for tea we have two slices of bread, butter and jam. Tuesdays, jam, butter and two slices of bread, and so on. The alternatives are—Cane syrup. At noons we always have bully beef and potatoes. Breakfasts oatmeal and ham fat. Its a wonderful.

I think Im doing very well. I've had two letters from you and one from Dad and Phil. I concluded from your letter yesterday that youve sent me some candy. I certainly hope it comes, for I am living on chocolate. I just cant eat the food they give us unless I am terribly hungry. I can live on nothing, however, so I dont worry at all. These Canadians are wonderful to me. So easy to get along with. They are very unselfish and good natured

There is another Mississippian here, a fellow who has been in the Delta, at Leland. He knows John Rainey.

I suppose Phil has left by now. It takes so long to get mail from home that things happen and then unhappen by the time I hear of them. And that child, Pat Houston, married! War is certainly hell, isn't it?

I'm having such a hurried life that all my letters sound disjointed. However!

Love
Billy

To Mrs. M. C. Faulkner   Wednesday [24 July 1918]
[env]   [Toronto]

The Candy and the Post came today And I've been
having one great time. I intend to make 3 meals off of that.

I am room orderly again today. I mopped the floor and
straightened the bunks. The officer commanding came and
inspected this morning.

I dont have to drill at all today, I have only to stay in the
room all day, for which I am deeply grateful, for they drilled
me yesterday until I was limping. These army boots are
ruining my feet.

Unless something happens I shall make a flight tomorrow
morning. If I do I shall write you to-morrow and tell you
about it.

Its rather warm here. I have to sweep about once an hour,
so I am continually in a gentle perspiration. This is wonderful candy.

Billy

To Mrs. M. C. Faulkner   Sunday [28 July 1918]
[env]   [Long Branch]

Dear Mother and Dad

We have been moved at last, and I've been so busy that
I've not had time to write since Thursday. Friday morning
we were inspected by the O.C., at noon we put on our walking out clothes and were inspected again, then marched to
the carline. This is what I carried—One overcoat, weight 15
lb, two kit bags, at 25 each, one suit case, at 20 lb, and one
stick.

They had special cars for us, and so we went through
Toronto singing Pack up your troubles in Your Old Kit

Bag, and Where do we go from here. We got to Long Branch, loaded down like pack mules and were inspected again.

This camp is on the bank of Lake Ontario and so we go swimming in the lake every day. Its very pretty to see the big lake steamers going up and down. I have a tent with two other cadets and a bed—BED—to sleep on. I've been sleeping on a board so much that I couldnt sleep at all the first night. The food here is much better and I am eating like a horse. There are planes in the sky all the time and the camp is full of English N.C.O's who say "'ave" and "ight" and "lite" instead of eight and late.

They have racing shells on the lake and they have track meets here and make us go in them. All new men are put on fatigues—which means work—for the first two weeks. Yesterday I was in the Mechanical Transport, riding back and forth to Toronto—about 20 miles—in a big truck. Tomorrow I'll probably be Cook 'ouse Charlie, or valet to some officer's tent. You never can tell. This is a wonderful place, just as cool. I am going to the lake to swim this afternoon.

Love
Billy

I passed my wireless exam, all right. This is my new address:

> Cadet William Faulkner
> ~~173799 Cadet Wing, Ro~~
> 173799 A Company, Flight 1
> Cadet Wing, Royal Air Force,
> Long Branch, Ontario, Canada

There is a bunch of mail at Jessie Ketcham for me. Hope they forward it today

To Mrs. M. C. Faulkner ?
[env]   [postmarked 31 July 1918]
                                             [Long Branch]

Dear Mother:
   3 letters today and a notice of a registered package. My
sweater, I hope. The weather now is about like our Novem-
bers. A Company has moved—A Co. did the moving, too.
Did more work yesterday than any Wop or Nigger living.
Slept like a log last night, woke up once and piled my kit
bags, tunic, overcoat, shoes and stick on me. Had my
clothes on all the time.
   My tent now faces the lake and I can watch the vessels
going up and down the lake, and the gulls like blown bits of
dirty paper.
   Some one has made a mistake, for we've been off 1 hour.
Calling us now, however, so I'm off.

                                             [no signature]

To Mrs. M. C. Faulkner   Wednesday [31 July 1918]
[env]   [Long Branch]

Dear Mother and Dad
   I have gotten more mail lately than any one in the camp
or the Flying Corps, for that matter. I average about 4 a day,
and one of my tent mates, a chap who transferred from the
Army Service Corps, said, Gee, Faulkner, some one is certainly in love with you. And I told him that some one was,
two for that matter.
   Today is a holiday. Which means that instead of drilling
today I've been working about twelve hours already. The
four Companies, A, B, C and D, are having a track meet and

I didn't get in, as all I can do is swim or play golf or bridge. The camp is open and full of visitors—Cadets mothers and fathers out to see them. There are cars coming in all the time and I am just thinking how good it would be to see you come through the gates in the "fliv," as dad said in his letter yesterday. However, letters are the next best thing, so I am in my tent with mine, and admiring the sweater which came today. Its the softest thing I ever had on. They make us wear our summer kits with frost every morning, and Ive been wearing my issue sweater under my shirt—we are not allowed to wear it on top, or our tunic either—because it doesn't scratch as much as the underclothes they issue us. But you can imagine how a sweater would feel next your skin, so you know how good the soft one feels.

I am keeping my underclothes, shirts socks and shoes, for, in 4 weeks, when we are sent to the S. of A.—School of Aeronautics, we have officers' tunics and can wear what we like.

John can wear the suit, and you might give the hat to Mammy, provided Dean doesn't want it. It would set either of them off. I am sitting in the sun with my shirt open so every one can see my sweater. Wish I could see you.

Billy

To Mrs. M. C. Faulkner   Saturday [3 Aug. 1918]
[env]   [Long Branch]

Dear Mother and Dad

I got paid yesterday—$12.00. They kept the rest to pay for my uniform. I'll get it back, however, when I get my new one. Ill have to spend about half of this on my walking-out shoes this afternoon. We have leave until 11:45 Monday night. I think I shall go down to Niagara on the steamer.

Its still cold. Every so often I feel inside my shirt to touch my sweater, and laugh.

I wish you could see the lake. I sit and look out over it and imagine I see Indian canoes going up and down, and deer and moose coming down and swimming out into the sunset, or fleets of bateaux filled with the soldiers of Marquis de Montcalm going down to Champlain, with the French and Huron Scouts flashing back and forth. In the morning, at sunrise, the lake is pink. Its easy then to imagine you see thin spirals of smoke from wigwams in front of which some befeathered warrior is making his prayers to the sun.

The night here are wonderful. There are lots of trees, that look like poured ink, with stiff, sharp pine trees, as though they had been cut from paper and stuck upon the sky. We see wild geese nearly every sunset. Its queer to be here and think of what this old lake has carried upon it. The Hurons and Iroquois fought all about here. I am acquiring the prettiest mahogany color you ever saw. I'll look like a pair of fashionable shoes soon.

Billy

To Mrs. M. C. Faulkner   Saturday P.M.
[env]   [10 Aug. 1918]
                                  [Long Branch]

Ive been so busy this week that I havent had time to write We have Saturday afternoons off, however, hence my chance. We are forbidden to say anything about this place, but Ive come in every night too tired to think even. In spite of the fact that I cant eat the food we get, Ive gained seven pounds. I weigh 127 now. More than I ever did. And I'll be so sunburned that I'll look like a nigger by Xmas.

I am going down town this afternoon and I shall have a picture made to send you. I got the money. Helps along marvellously. There is a certain Widder lady who runs a place near here where we can get milk and good food and eggs—eggs! Havent seen an egg in so long that I wouldn't even know a lady chicken from a gentleman one.

That was a splendid picture of John. It came yesterday, with a letter you wrote me about the middle of July. So there's no saying how many letters of yours I've never gotten, nor how many of mine have never reached you. This is the first week I've missed writing every day. Had a card from Phil from Providence, R.I. yesterday

Lieut. Todd is here. He is going to help me a lot.

This is certainly an immoral place. I have had stolen to wit: My stick, razor, mirror and brushes, knife, fork and spoon, and a pair of putties. I am going to nail every thing else I have to the floor.

Billy

To Mrs. M. C. Faulkner   Sunday [11 Aug. 1918]
[env]   [Long Branch]

Mother and Dad

I got two letters yesterday—the three dollar one and the ten dollar one, so I went down last night and had these taken. I've got four. I'm sending you one apiece, and grandfather one. They are not much, for this is my "rookie" uniform and was literally thrown at me. I'll not get my sure enough one until I get to the S. of A.—school of gunnery, aerial fighting, etc—when my eight weeks are up. As soon as I can, Ill send one in my summer clothes, and one standing beside a 'plane, you know, egregious; with one hand resting carressingly and protectively upon its knee cap.

The money is great, and I look forward every week to the post. I can buy 'em myself, now, though. And please send me one bath towel and that thin book of poems with the French grey cover—Poems, by Ralph Hodgson[1]—and the socks and helmet will be great when it turns cold here. I have one that fits over my head and across my mouth.

I feel better today than I have in quite a while. Just returned from Church of England services. They are about the same as our Episcopal. My new uniform will be like this. [FIGURE][2]

Billy

I've got an aluminum disc on my right wrist, like this. [FIGURE][3]

---

[1]English Georgian poet (1871–1962). Faulkner apparently sent Hodgson's *Poems* to Estelle Oldham Franklin in 1918 or the following year inscribed with lines he later incorporated into his verse play *The Marionettes*.

[2]Line drawing of a flying officer in jodhpurs and belted tunic with stick.

[3]Line drawing of an oval identification braclet bearing the R.A.F. seal, the name "Wm Faulkner," and the number 173799.

To Mrs. M. C. Faulkner   Monday [12 Aug. 1918]
[env]   [Long Branch]

Mother darling

I just got your letter and I'm home sick for the first time. It all began Saturday night. I was down town at the King Edward Hotel with Lieut. Todd, and as I came out, a newsee came up right in front of me. He was like a little sparrow, with a tiny bird voice, and he looked exactly like Sweet,[1] bless his heart, snaggled toothed; I could almost see the speckled cap and hear him whistling "Good bye now." I told him I didnt want a paper, but he stood and showed me that gap in his mouth for a moment, then reached in his jacket and gave me a stick of chewing gum. Of course I bought a paper then, and gave him a dime. A Canadian nickle is about this size—[FIGURE]² —and when I handed him the dime I gave him two of them without knowing it. He tried to give me back fifteen cents of it, but I refused, so he gave me three more sticks of gum, whereupon I took him down and bought him a pink ice-cream soda. And I've been wanting to see Dean so much since that I almost dream about him every night.

Its probably well that I was not within walking distance of home when I received your letter, or I'd be on my way. As for doing anything foolish, I wouldnt miss the chance of coming home like a "bloomin' dook" to show our worthy compatriots what a chap I am, by heating myself up. They dont do things like that here, anyway.

I havent cashed my two other money orders yet—the 2.50 and the 10.00 ones. Keeping them to sleep on. A Company has become quite military now. Some of them, however, still salute the sergeant-major.

Love you, Momsey

Here is one of the pictures I had made to go on my papers when I enlisted. It's strange how much younger this uniform makes us look. We are like boy scouts in our summer outfits. I look about 25 here.

[no signature]

---

¹Dean Swift Falkner, Faulkner's youngest brother. His twelfth birthday was August 15.

²Line drawing of a coin, one-quarter inch in diameter.

To Mrs. M. C. Faulkner   Thursday [15 Aug. 1918]
[env]   [Long Branch]

I am going to buy me a pair of dress shoes—walking-out
shoes, they call them here—and a pair of dress putties with
my $12.50. The other day some of the cadets here made
such a kick about the food that they have changed the system. The food is better cooked and we can have as much as
we want now, instead of a single plateful, like they used to
give us.

The camp is on the outskirts of a summer colony, a park
and dances every night. I havent danced any yet, however,
not having any shoes. Its impossible to dance in the army
shoes. They have "iron" soles with hobnails in them something like this—[FIGURE][1]
I have met a very attractive girl who has a summer home in
Long Branch, so now I have something to do with my holidays—Wednesdays and Saturdays and Sundays from 5
until 12 o'clock. I was down ~~She had me down Sunday~~ Sunday afternoon and she kept me to tea—they all (over. Run
out of paper) OVER have tea here every afternoon. Even we
do)—and then walked back to camp with me and went
home on the street car. Her name is Allen.

Did you get the picture I sent?

[no signature]

---

[1]Line drawing of a hobnail boot.

To Mrs. M. C. Faulkner   Sunday [18 Aug. 1918]
[env]   [Long Branch]

Dear Mother and Dad

I bought me a pair of shoes yesterday—got them from Minster's, the best place in Toronto, but I have a sample sized foot No 7, I got th a sample pair. Very nice shoes and cost $7.00. I used the other three of my ten for a pair of putties. Now I dont look as though I had on two suit cases with pieces of flannel wrapped around my legs.

It is perfect weather up here, crisp and clear and cold as time at night. The summer is over, and last night we could see the Aurora Borealis. It certainly looked queer, like a search light. It didnt flicker at all, and about half way up the sky we could see the shadow of the flat end of the earth at the pole.[1]

I have been out this morning watching Captain Leigh doing stunts in a brand new plane. I wish you could be here today. You know how trees rustle in the wind Thats exactly the way the lake sounds like tearing tissue paper. I can sit in my tent and see two vessels twelve or fourteen miles out, and back of me there are seven planes in the air.

I am going out to th another flying camp this afternoon, the acrobatics school. Send the "Post" whenever you care to. Always enjoy it.

Love
Billy

[1]Faulkner enclosed with this letter a rough pencil sketch of the waves of light in the Aurora Borealis.

To Mrs. M. C. Faulkner   Thursday [22 Aug. 1918]
[env]   [Long Branch]

The towel and book came safely. One towel is enough, for I can wash it every sunday morning. Youd never guess the reason I havent written—because I had no stamps and no money, ran absolutely dry. And the funny part is, I still have the other two money orders—10 and 2.50. I couldn't cash them because they were made out on Long Branch, which is a summer colony about half an hours ride by trolley, too far to walk in the time off I've had since Monday. I had to get the post office here to send down for the receipts for them, and as soon as they come, I get my money. I certainly havent spent any money in the canteen this week, been eating at the mess hall every day. There is no form or fashion in which I can draw a draft here. I've gotten along remarkably well, however, on nothing. I lost my pipe the other day, and I've missed my smoking more than anything, for I've had tobacco but no cigarettes. I know a place in town where they are having a pipe sale and I am going to get one Saturday, for $1.00.

Am I to understand from your letter that John is at home? And Phil?

I can receive seven words a minute for four minutes in wireless now. I almost ~~hav~~ dream in dots and dashes ~~now~~. We also have a lecture every day in map making and reading, both in spite of the fact that I am a pilot-cadet and not an observer. My squadron commander is an observer, the wing commander, however, is a pilot, an ace who has nine Huns officially, Major Samson.

Had an awful storm on the lake last night. Rained in my tent so that I put all my stuff on my bed and slept under it. Kept warm, too. We still get up at 5:45. Before dawn, now. It will be snowing next. I look just like a kodak negative

now. All brown my self, and my hair is burned rope color.
[FIGURE][1]

Here is something that went with me my first time
"up" I have one on the shoulder of all̶y̶ my shirts and my
tunic I wrote the day my cheesecrackers and deviled ham
came and told you how much I liked it. Dare you to send me
something to eat now.

[no signature]

[1]Line drawing of a dark face with light hair.

To Mrs. M. C. Faulkner   Tuesday [27 Aug. 1918]
[env]   [Long Branch]

The cakes and two letters came yesterday and last night I
got some apples at the canteen, and a bottle of pop and ate
them—the cakes, not the letters— for supper. It turned cold
again last night. I thought I was seeing unseasonable
weather at New Haven, but it has gone absolutely wild here.
I am expecting snow before my birthday. They tell me it
usually snows here about the first of November.

Far be it from me to make guesses as to when I shall get
leave, for now the closer I stick, the sooner I shall get to
where the leave wouldnt throw me a month behind The
classes change every two weeks, and if I miss one, it means
waiting fourteen days for the next.

I got the money. Shall put it with my coming home fund.
I went to Toronto over the week end, just to get some sleep.

You mentioned very casually in your letter that Aunt
Willie is dead.[1] It rather pulled me up with a bump for your
letter—I suppose you wrote me before, hasn't come yet. I
am glad I̶ ̶d̶i̶d̶n̶t̶ you sent the flowers for me. When did it
happen? I seem to have marooned myself absolutely from
every thing up here.

I would like to see the kid, now. Growing like a weed, I suppose, and have some eggs and fried chicken and jelly and hot biscuit and peaches. Amen.

Billy

[1]Faulkner's paternal great-aunt, Willie Medora Falkner Carter, eldest daughter of the Old Colonel, William Clark Falkner (1825–1889).

To Mrs. M. C. Faulkner   Friday [30 Aug. 1918]
[env]   [Long Branch]

They are holding an Exhibition in Toronto,[1] and I think I'll go this week, when the holidays come. Its like the fair at Memphis, I suppose—Horses and cattle and peanuts and dogs that smell like children, and do not care, and children who smell like wet dogs, and who do not care any more than the dogs do. We are studying compasses and drawing maps now, as well as having wireless.

Got my post all right. I think I've gotten all the things you have sent, only a letter or so has gone astrey. Nothing startling has happened here lately, except the Company had its picture taken. Very much the same. We are up at before day now, the days are so much shorter.

I have something to look forward to now—we will leave here three weeks from today, back to Toronto, to study Aerial navigation.

Billy

[1]The Canadian National Exhibition, held annually in late August and early September in Toronto.

To Mrs. M. C. Faulkner   Sunday 1–18 [3 Sept. 1918]
[env]   [Long Branch]

The sweater, socks and cigs came yesterday, and Ive just gotten another package Havent opened it yet, but I have an idea its something to eat. I am feeling fine. I wish you could see how much I have gained. I took a look at myself in a mirror the other day and I am as round faced as John.

The sweater is going to come in quite handy, soon, I am thinking. The mornings and evenings are crisp now, and the northern lights were plainer than ever now. In another month they will begin shooting across the sky.

Last night I went to the exposition. Crowds and fireworks and smells. And bands and hurdy gurdies on all sides.

There was a 'plane from the aerobatics school at Beamsville over just now. Tomorrow is a holiday, and I am going out if I can and get one of the cadet-pilots I know to take me up.

My tent is full of people now, and as I do not care for people, I'm waiting until they go to open my box, and so I can divide with Reed and Del. (Delaney is the one I wrote you about—from Albany, N.Y, went to Pennsylvania to school and is a very nice chap)[1] He and I have managed to stick together so far. I refuse to give your cakes to every Tom and Dick in camp here. This crowd hangs about like a crowd of vultures, waiting until some one to get a box from home. If I were not naturally rather unapproachable, they'd take it away from me.

Had a letter from Grandfather. Tomorrow is his birthday.[2] I hope he gets his letter on time.

---

[1]Edward Delaney, a native of Mount Vernon, New York, attended Villanova University.

[2]J.W.T. Falkner, the Young Colonel, was born September 2, 1848.

To Mrs. M. C. Faulkner   Thursday [5 Sept. 1918]
[env]   [Long Branch]

Dear Mother and Dad

I cant realize that Jack is overseas.[1] Both of us have wanted to go so badly, and its queer to ~~see~~ know he's gotten there. What about Rodney and Ed Lewis? Did they go too? I certainly envy Jack the things he'll see, London and Paris. He'll probably ~~be~~ finish his training and be sent "up" about January—just in time to see the finish, and he will probably be put in line for a commission, most of the young ones are kept back and trained for officers. We must be sure and get his stuff to him Xmas. Let me know the date you send it so I can send something to go in the package.

We had another awful storm last night and my fingers are so cold I can hardly hold my pencil. I have on three sweaters and my overcoat when I go out

I sent the blue suit home about a month ago. Has it arrived yet? As for sending me things, I can get razor blades and soap at the canteen, its the papers and little things to eat that I love to get from home, especially the ones that you and Mammy cook. I wrote you the day the $5.00 came. You have probably gotten my letter by now.

And to think of old Jack coming back with a returned man's stripes! I am looking forward to the furlough I'll get before I go overseas, so we can talk about him.

Give Johnsy and Dean my love, and make 'em write me. My heart goes out to you both, and may God protect and shield you, darling mother and dad, just half as much as your love and prayers for Jackie will shield him.

Billy

[1]Jack Falkner landed in Brest in August with the 66thCompany of the 5th Regiment of Marines. He was wounded in fighting at the Argonne Forest November 1, 1918.

To Mr. M. C. Faulkner   Monday [9 Sept. 1918]
[env]   [Long Branch]

I'm having one hell of a time today, with a tooth. It had a cavity, but had not hurt me any. So today I decided to have it fixed, went down this morning and he has started taking the nerve out, and its raising the wind now. I can see my self sitting up all to night. The darned thing has got the whole side of my face and head hurting.

The ginger cake sounds good, and the oatmeal cookies ~~good~~ too. I'll certainly be glad when my tooth is fixed for I cant eat anything now. I'm going to write a better letter than this when my tooth stops, just now its going 60 an hour, on all cylinders.

The things you sent were very good   Here is one I've done for the Cadet Wing Review ~~on the back~~

My address is now

> A Company Flight 3
> Cadet Wing, R.A.F.

                            [no signature]

THE ACE[1]

The silent earth looms blackly in the dawning
Sharp as poured ink beneath the grey
Mists spectral, clutching fingers
                    The sun light
Paints him as he stalks, huge through the morning
In his fleece and leather, and gilds his bright
Hair. The first lark hovers, singing, where
He flashes through the shining gates of day.

---

[1]There are two variant holograph fragments of "The Ace," one of which is transcribed in Faulkner's 1918 R.A.F. notebook. This version combines modified parts of both.

To Mrs. M. C. Faulkner   Thursday 12 [Sept. 1918]
[env]   [Long Branch]

Dear Mother and Dad

According to custom, it rained Wednesday, so it is warmer again, warm enough to be comfortable with only 2 sweaters. It was so cold Tuesday night that it had to do something I expected snow my self. We have laid away our boy scout suits now, thank heaven, and I am far more comfortable. I have had two teeth filled, another tomorrow. Captain Leonard, the dentist, has found so many things wrong with my teeth that I had no idea of, that I am not going back after tomorrow. He is a good dentist, though. Only one of them hurt me, the one he removed the nerve from.

We are all mud to the knees today. Still carrying on, however. If you could see me wading around in the water and mud, and sleeping any way, wet clothes or not, you'd have a fit, Mother, any way would. It doesnt hurt me, I go down before dawn and eat my oatmeal and beef stew like a little man.

The ginger cakes came yesterday and I et 'em forthwith, also three banannas, and ice cream cone and a chocolate bar. The peppermint candy I saved and ate before breakfast this morning. Now—4:00—I have eaten four pieces of dry bread, preparatory to tea at 5:30, after which I'll probably buy some cookies at the canteen to exist on until morning. It's dark when we get up now. We have lanterns in the tents. Cosy and much warmer than you'd think.

The posting comes off next week—Friday. The S. of A. takes 200 cadets every two weeks, and as our Company is large—268, I am trusting to luck that I'll be one of the lucky ones. I passed my wireless examination— 6 words for 3 min-utes 6 words a minute for 3 minutes, perfect—yesterday.

About half the Co. failed. They are Confined to Barracks—
no passes at all—until they pass. I am fairly good at wireless
though. O

About those leggings. No one except a commissioned officer is allowed to wear them (excepting the Motorcycle
Corps men) so I cant h even keep them, much less wear
them, much as I would like to. I had a letter from Johnsy
today. I am answering it to morrow, and I'll try to send him
a cap.

Has my suit ever gotten home? I sent it some time ago,
wrote you at the time, and have a receipt for it. Let me know
and I'll try to trace it.

I am in fairish spirits since my tooth stopped hurting.

If those gray buckskin gloves of mine are there, please
send them to me. If not, I shall buy some here.

I dont doubt you not being able to read this. I tried just
then and couldnt, myself. What they need here is a penman-
ship class.

Worlds of love

Billy

Address

A Squadron Flight 3
Cadet Wing R.A.F.

I might be ragged and full of fleas
But my pants, thank God, dont bag at the knees.

Cheer-O

To Mrs. M. C. Faulkner   Sunday [15 Sept. 1918]
[env]   [Long Branch]

I think every time I write home, it is to say—Such and such a thing arrived safely, but I believe I do get something every day, so there is nothing for me to need. The two ~~po~~ magazines came the same day, and it rained this morning, so I am having a debauch of literature. Queer to think of my contenting myself with such simple joys as 'Hearsts' and the Post. I got your letter saying my clothes had come and that John is wearing them.

It rains now every day, very methodical and very damp, with a queer, impervious detachment, worthier of a far better cause than that of producing gelatinous mud in such quantities. I am very fortunate in having a small lake form behind my hut, so that when I come off parade with my boots muddy to my waist, I take my broom, wade out in the lake and wash 'em off. C'est la vie de la vie! if you gather my meaning.

The people up here all think that I am French, from Montreal, for some reason. I am watching for better weather, so I can get my friend at the flying camp to take me up again. Lieutenant Todd will be in flying camp shortly, then I'll probably be able to make lots of flights with him.

I certainly will be glad to get home, I have so many things and people to talk about, the cockney Non Commissioned officers here, and so forth.

I am hoping to be with the posted out bunch on Friday. I'll have better quarters and food and every thing.

Something to do now, of course, so I must carry on.

Billy

To Mrs. M. C. Faulkner Tuesday [17 Sept. 1918]
[env]   [Long Branch]

We are preparing to leave Friday—provided we pass our tests and are one of the lucky ones. There are more in the Squadron than the S of A will take, so there is no way of being certain. Had two wireless tests this morning—sending and receiving.

I had a letter from Phil yesterday. He told me of Edison Avent's[1] grief over being rejected, and about Katrina with her job in New York.[2]

I certainly will be glad if I go Friday. Nearer my home coming, and the end of the hard part of the course. We have six weeks at the S of A, and if we are sent overseas then, we get leave to go home. It is something like a girls finishing school, teaches us not to eat with our knives, and trifles like that; lest we disgrace the King's Commission that we hope to receive.

The mail just came, with Jacks address, and the package. I wrote you last week, and told you that we are not allowed to wear leather leg coverings of any sort, only officers wear boots and leather putties.

Mr. ~~Stewart~~ Fletcher, the O.C.—Major Hodgin's—aid, has a soft job, rides around behind the Major all day, sort of a human hot water bottle, to keep the proletariat, or great un-washed; one of which I am whom, from touching him. And by the way, in this army, a lieutenant is called Mr So-and-so, not by his title. ~~W~~ To continue, this morning Mr Fletcher was galloping along over this water-soaked part of the earth, and his mount went down with him. Very exciting, to him anyway, for he has doubtless done more graceful things. He was not hurt, however, came up all over mud.

I havent been out of camp for over a week now, so I dont

know any scandal. I am going out now and wash my shoes off before they call a parade on me.

Billy

¹T. E. Avent, subsequently a cashier in the First National Bank of Oxford owned originally by Faulkner's grandfather, J.W.T. Falkner.

²In 1917–1918 Katrina Carter served as a YMCA canteen worker, first in Washington and then in New York.

To Mrs. M. C. Faulkner Thursday [19 Sept. 1918]
[env] [Long Branch]

We are going to-morrow, so I'll not be able to write to-morrow at all. You can have visions of me walking 1/4 mile carrying the following: 1 overcoat, 2 kit bags, one haversack, 1 cork helmet, 1 pair of boots, 1 stick, 1 suit case. I'll look like an immigrant for sure.

Golly, but I'm glad to go! Good food, good quarters, no drills, just lecturing, acquiring knowledge in the gentle art of gunnery for boches. The S of A is the University of Toronto, in town instead of being in the woods like the Cadet Wing.

I've been interviewed and inoculated and vaccinated and categoried already this morning. To morrow afternoon we go out. The band plays for us and the other squadrons stand to attention when we pass. It seems years ago that I came here, and saw the other A Squadron go out, and now at last we go out, to look on the rookies who come in to morrow with supercilious condescention.

Any mail that comes to me at the Cadet Wing will be forwared to S of A. I'll send my new address as soon as I am given one—going up for mail now—which reminds me again of that cake. I ate all the big pieces, then took the crumbs with a spoon. I am going in town tonight and I shall weigh again. I believe I'm still gaining I can go down to breakfast in the morning and eat a bowl of oatmeal, some beef stew and bread, come out with a slice of bread and butter, and stop at the canteen for two muffin cakes, I can eat cheese any time, and candy before breakfast, and I'd give my right eye for some scrambled eggs and toast and Kraft cheese and jelly and fried chicken and peaches.

School of Aeronautics tomorrow!

Billy

To Mrs. M. C. Faulkner   Saturday [21 Sept. 1918]
[env]   [Toronto]

Dear Mother

I am moved at last. The address is:

Cadet Wm. F.
173799, Course 42
4 School of Aeronautics, Royal Air Force
University of Toronto, Canada

As usual we are not to divulge any information, but I can say that I certainly do like this place, wish I could spend the winter here instead of six weeks.

The food is absolutely wonderful, after the Cadet Wing. We are living in th a dormitory,[1] will have steam heat and electricity. I cant get over the food, though. Clean table clothes and china, china, mind you. Women cooks, and milk and sugar, and dessert for lunch and dinner. From now on my growth will be visible to the naked eye.

This place is quite like New Haven or Yale. I mean, it has

an air which is quite English and quite ugly. The buildings, some of them, are individually attractive enough, but they are so terribly out of taste, sort of red-faced, beef-and-cheese tastlessness. Its very pretty, though, now that fall is here and the leaves are turning.

Shall write more to morrow, when I have time. The money came safely. Am going to buy gloves with it.

Billy

---

[1]Faulkner was quartered at Wycliffe College, the University of Toronto.

To Mrs. M. C. Faulkner   Monday [23 Sept. 1918]
[env]   [Toronto]

~~B. E. or C.~~

The longer I am here the better I like it. No more rifle drills and fatigue parties now. We are at lectures all day, wireless classes and theory of flight and airplane construction and it is very interesting. Like being in school again, only the subjects are not dry-as-dust abstract things, like x = the angle of an isosceles triangles so many degrees, and so on, or stuff like what a certain herb found in India will do to the liver of a man who has spent most of his life at the north pole.

The meals are still splendid. After what they gave me to eat up to this time, I'd do any thing in the world for any man, woman, child or Chinaman who would feed me like this. Think of scrambled eggs for breakfast. Oh, boy!

I am in Toronto now, not hell-and-gone in the country. Will be here about six weeks.

Get Grandfather to show you the snap shot of my squadron I sent him. Oh, yes, I have risen in the world. Before I was ~~a 3A Canada~~ 173799 Canada *3* AM Cadet for Pilot, and now I am, reading from left to right:

173799 Canada 2 AM Cadet for Pilot.
Next I will be
173799 Canada Cadet-Pilot

Just a glance at that one would think I had been decorated. However, this is the life, and thank God we have a navy.

Your last letter said you hadnt heard from me in quite a while. I am going to start putting my address on the envelopes. I cant blame the P.O. people for missending them, for when I try to read my writing I never know whether its English or Sanscrit.

Billy

To Mrs. M. C. Faulkner   Wednesday [25 Sept. 1918]
[env]   [Toronto]

Dear Mother and Dad

The wire came today.[1] First mail I've gotten since I came here. It is forwarded from Cadet Wing, but I suppose our recent manoeuvers have balled things up more or less, and the mail will come in time.

We went out to flying camp[2] yesterday afternoon, and I learned how to crank an aero motor by swinging the propeller. I was rather surprised when I did it. It's rather scary though, the thing goes off with such a roar. Saw lots of flying, as yesterday was very clear, a great flying day.

Having a great little time, though we get up earlier here than at Long Branch   Still I can do an awful lot on the food here, which is absolutely Non Plush Ultra.

It was too bad that Lieut. Todd left here just two weeks before I came in. I could have seen him oftener, though. In this army an officer is not allowed to pal around with a private, still, now that I am out of ground school and learning how to act like an officer, it would have been all right.

It's certainly strange, the difference in the way an American officer can play about with an private while up here they ignore each other.

> I love you.
> Billy
> "Mr" William Falkner

Give John birthday wishes for me,[3] and love to Dean.

[1]Probably containing birthday wishes. September 25 was Faulkner's twenty-first birthday.
[2]Leaside Airport north of Toronto.
[3]John Falkner's seventeenth birthday was September 24.

To Mrs. M. C. Faulkner   Saturday 28 [Sept. 1918]
[env]   [Toronto]

Dear Mother and Dad

The cake came and I'll say it was good. I have made more friends with pieces of it than you'd ever think possible. None of my letters from Long Branch have come for some reason, though I got one today from you addressed here and written on my birthday. Phil's cigs havent come yet, however. I have just finished the pieces of icing on it. I eat so much here that I never buy things in the canteen like I did at the Cadet Wing, fact, I practically lived in the canteen there. I have John's cap I promised him, and I shall send it as soon as I can get out and get some stamps. As it is, I have only three.

I imagine Jack is having one great time over there, doubtless he and Joe Pegues havent time to play cards now.

dammit, I wish I could get my mail from Long Branch. I couldnt get any Thursday—last week, we left Friday noon, and up until you got my first letter from here there must have accumulated some any way. And I hate to think of some of those —. —*! cockney corporals and sergeants smoking my good cigarettes.

The work here is very interesting. I wish they allowed us to go into detail about it. We have all sorts of engines, map reading wireless, artillery observation.

Our squadron is not allowed off the campus for some reason now,[1] and I dont know when I'll get some more stamps, so so it may be 2 or 3 days before I can write again, as I have canvassed the building thoroughly for stamps to send John's cap to him. The Kid is an older man now too, isnt he? Tell him I say to carry on at school and write me often.

About my furlough. It is indefinite. If I am picked to go overseas at the end of my course here, I'll be notified in time to make every thing, if I am not picked, I'll be kept here indefinitely unless you send me a wire saying you are ill or some thing. I will write as soon as I know if I'll be taken or not. I am am sent overseas I will be given a commission at on the steamer.

Thank you for the cake. I wish it had come today instead of yesterday.

Billy

[1]During most of the fall of 1918, the School of Aeronautics, like all of Toronto, was under quarantine because the Spanish influenza epidemic.

To Mrs. M. C. Faulkner　　　Thursday [3 Oct. 1918]
[env]　　　　　　　　　　　[Toronto]

Dear Mother and Dad

We have just finished our daily ten miles. The band— which can play only one tune, an ancient English parish hymn syncopated to something resembling march time—

playing to beat time, with the usual complement of small boys about the kid's size. I certainly will be glad when this quarantine lifts and we resume classes. I am absolutely fed up with marching. The officers go along with us, and often come in on a run in spite of the king's commissions.

The fields here are full of purple and yellow flowers, and all the brick walls are covered with crimson flowers of some kind, and red and yellow leaves. All the trees are turning, and by comparison the spruce and pine looks black. There are some trees here that bear red berries about like plums, called haws, the things wild animals are always eating in stories of Canada. I'd give any thing in the world for a horse to ride now. This is a sure enough Indian summer. Dad would be crazy about this country, everything is so pretty now, almost as colorful as our falls, and it lasts so much longer.

I sent you a snap shot a fellow made of me, in my cadet uniform and white band, with a false white beard and tinted spectacles, to show you how the life agreed with me. I expected it to create a commotion, but as I haven't heard from you, I dont suppose you got it. It looked like this, was good I thought— [FIGURE][1] I imagine I must have looked like Mr. Leake in a boy scout uniform.

This is the worst war I was ever in. And ten miles to-morrow staring me in the face!

Billy

No mail from Long Branch yet.

---

[1]Line drawing of a cadet in summer uniform with white beard and dark glasses.

To Mrs. M. C. Faulkner   Sunday [6 Oct. 1918]
[env]   [Toronto]

There is a Red Cross nurse in the hospital who eats in our mess hall, who holds the King's commission as a first lieutenant, has her pips on her shoulders, and the gold bar with Canada in it like an officer. We salute her, also, just like an officer. She returns the salute by nodding her head. She has been overseas.

I sent John his cap. If he has sold all his army stuff, tell him to let Dean wear it, or Sallie. She wanted one and I could only send my old one, as we are allowed only two.

All my long Branch mail came finally, three letters.

It is raining to beat time today. Nothing to do, so I have been in a bridge game which netted me $8.10. Not bad, for one afternoon's playing or working. The quarantine has not lifted yet, there are rumors that it will go through next week. I wish I had a speedometer on me, just to know how far I have walked since last Sunday.

That was clever, Dad, what you wrote about Phil, ~~rather~~ ~~[illegible]~~ you let Phil have it straight though, for I believe the poor devil really feels bad about being around home. Just wait until you see the kid and Phil and me raise hell on our furlough.

Mother says Dean walks you to death every Sunday. Dean is in the wrong army. He should be in this one. We average ten miles per day ~~se~~ for the last six days, not counting 2 1/2 hours drill in the morning. When I wake up at reveille, I hear first off—"'Shun! Stand at ease! As you were! Move to the right in fours, form fours, right! Quick-march!"

And I go to bed with my legs so tired my neck hurts. I havent been out to fly any m in about 3 weeks.

Billy

P.S. As for writing often, I wish I had more time to write you all

To Mrs. M. C. Faulkner   11 A.M. Thursday
[env]   [10 Oct. 1918]
                                            [Toronto]

The cake came. It is the first cake—I mean chocolate cake—I've had since I left home. The Canadian idea of a good hot dessert—some of ye olde stuffe—is corn syrup and corn muffins. Honest, we have that lots. And you will not believe it, but the sort of cake they give you with a dessert of fruit is hot biscuit. Its the only time they ever eat them, consider them quite a delicacy. So I sit up and tell 'em about peaches and fried chicken and hot biscuits for breakfast in the south and they are all for moving there. I have got one piece of the cake that I'm saving, to eat a little at a time.

I think I told you that I had learned to drink milk—well the eight of us at my table this morning drank 3 gallons. We have all the milk and wheat bread we want, and we are the only people in Toronto who have white sugar. The *! —- * quarantine has not been lifted yet.

The O.C. of my squadron is Scotch, Lieutenant McAlister, I wish you could see him, he is absolutely astounding looking, kinds of numbs you to look at him, leaves a queer dead feeling as though an electric shock had passed through you. He looks exactly like that fellow who plays with Chaplin some time—the one with no chin and the cross eyes.[1]

The Keystone people would have given his father $1000 for him cash in hand, on the day of his birth. [FIGURE][2]

No, I cannot use the camera at all.

Yes, I cant have too many socks.

Grandfather's letter returned home at last. It was sent to Oxford, Massachusettes ~~the [illegible]~~ then back to me, and as it was more or less man handled, I am writing him another one today.

6 P.M. We have just finished our ten miles and I am very near all in—too tired to eat, all most. Pay parade comes off tonight and I'll chase over and collect my $7.00. Lord knows what I'll do with it, as I can spend it now.

Still later—this is becoming a diary. Already sounds like an Elynor Glyn[3] story where the heroine sits in her boudoir, gazing at her reflection in the mirror and pulls off 5,734 words of introspection—you know. One of these subdued, mahogany and ivory stories with his ~~high~~ grace kissing the upper parlor maid in the butler's pantry.

At the mess call on the bugle my fatigue abated enough to allow me to partake of a little nourishment, whereupon I descended, ate roast beef and potatoes and cabbage and ice cream, purchased three apples in the canteen and ate the remainder of the crumbs of cake icing. Chased over and was paid. Will buy 100 1¢ stamps as soon as the canteen opens again, later will play bridge with an Englishman from China who knows the Mr Reed I knew in New Haven, who wrote me the character recommendation.

I have almost outgrown my B.V.D's and smoke only four times per day—sometimes none. I wish I'd get sick or break a spring or something, so I could not walk every afternoon.

I Ħ am lying on my bed now. They are having an eternal parade very noisily in the street 3 stories down, quite dusk now. There is a very ugle massive white building across from me, suspended like a giant soap bubble in a grove of trees, sure enough scarlet trees, which absorb light all day until in the dusk they are slightly luminous. Gosh! I wish Dad could see this country! We could sleep out every night, the underbrush is soft as moss. All you need is a blanket. And there are no varmints.

This is how I looked when I came out of Jessie Ketcham barracks. [FIGURE][4]

Billy

---

[1]The actor was Ben Turpin.

[2]Line drawing of a Scots lieutenant in kilts and tam with a heavy mustache.

[3]English novelist Elinor Glyn (1861–1943), whose public popularity rested upon slightly scandalous romances such as *The Vicissitudes of Evangeline* (1905) and *Three Weeks* (1907).

[4]Line drawing of a cadet in uniform.

To Mrs. M. C. Falkner   Sunday [13 Oct. 1918]
[env]   [Toronto]

The quarantine has not lifted yet. My hair is so long that I am going to powder it and put a black satin ribbon on it. We are still supported in the style to which we were not accustomed at the Cadet Wing.   life continues on the even tenor of its way, days of eating and sleeping and full of egregious stupidity, like "Curfew shall not ring tonight" or ~~some mes~~ Longfellow meandering through a perfect autumn day in one of his astonishingly vapid effusions.

There are some kids in the street below, raising the wind. One of them sounds like Sweet when he's fussing and jawing at Jack or mammy.

I neglected to go on the route march this afternoon, as I was on picket duty last night. The parade is just returning, headed by that agglomeration of flatted discords which some enthusiast, in a moment of uncontrollable excitement, called a ~~[illegible]~~ band.

I wrote Grandfather yesterday. Let me know if he got it, so I can try again to foil the Postal System. Every time I get a letter home to you, I feel a certain pleasurable glow of exultation, as though I had downed a Hun machine.

Did John get his cap?

Billy

P.S: What do you know about it, the Canadian thanksgiving is tomorrow. Dreadfully out of place, I think.

Give mammy my love. Am going to send her a card this week.

To Mrs. M. C. Faulkner   Monday [14 Oct. 1918]
[env]   [Toronto]

Dear Madam—

In reply to yours of the ? inst. please send me one tube of Pekco tooth paste and a kiss from the kid. Canadian tooth paste, like Canadian tobacco, is flat as stale beer.

Classes opened today, thank goodness, but the quarantine has not. My hair is now curling attractively over the collar of my tunic. Even the girl who sells tickets in the canteen thinks I need a haircut.

I have lots of fun with the French Canadians here. They usually think I am French, and I can walk up to any of them ~~and~~ with a cigarette and say— [~~["illegible] feu de [illegible]"~~ ~~"[illegible]" "[illegible] feu de [illegible]"~~ "voulez vous la

ses allume?" and they take me up at once. I dont last long,
however, but its great sport while it lasts.

Billy

To Mrs. M. C. Falkner Thursday [17 Oct. 1918]
[env] [Toronto]

Mother Darling

The magazine came—finally. All the Flying Corps
trucks—light ones, with seats along the sides and usually
Fords, for carrying Cadets back and forth, ~~are~~ to flying
camp, are driven by girls and they wear the caps and tunics,
~~sa~~ like the girl's picture on the mag. Janice George, the
actress, was in Toronto last summer, and some cadet became very much enamoured of her and gave her a complete
R.A.F. uniform, and she wore it in one of her plays this fall.

There are ~~so~~ quite a lot of celebrities in my course here.
Almost every where you turn you see service chevrons on a
sleeve—like this, just above the wrist. [FIGURE][1] A blue
stripe for every year or portion thereof, and a red one for
nineteen fourteen. Two of the corporals—cadet corporals—
were in the Princess Pats at Ypres, April 28, 1915. They are
two of the very few who returned, and both of them are
Americans.

One of them Kavanaugh, from Los Angeles, spent 4 days
in Suicide ditch at the lip of the Ypres salient, without food
or water. Wears two wound stripes. And the cadet sergeant
of the squadron has the Military Medal, looks like this—
[FIGURE][2] He was a sniper. Officially credited with 43
Huns. He was bringing in a wounded "venate" under fire
and a shell got him.

Another corporal, named [Youreys ?] was over three
years—Somme and Vimy ridge, and has never worn a pair

of long civilian trousers. was in short pants when he enlisted. His father and brother went and so did he, until his
mother made the Government send him home.

Quarantine has lifted. We are ~~confined~~ at classes again,
and the irony is, they lifted quarantine because King's Regulations and Orders says you cant hold classes under quarantine, so they merely Confined us to Barracks which is
utterly the same thing. So you see, there is more than one
way to skin a cat.

I am still getting fat. I'll have to start reducing soon. I
dont look like this yet, however. [FIGURE][3]

Billy

[1]Line drawing of a service chevron with two stripes.
[2]Line drawing of the Military Medal.
[3]Line drawing of an overweight cadet in uniform.

To Mrs. M. C. Faulkner   Monday [21 Oct. 1918]
[env]   [Toronto]

The quarantine has not lifted yet, though one can parade
for a pass to see a dying relative or some such thing. I am
saving up, for it is customary, before a cadet is sent overseas, to give him indefinite leave, which means that he is
called up again when they are needed, anywhere from seven
to seventeen days, and as I am so far from home, I may be
they will give me an extension. I hope so, any way. I would
be great if I could be home for Christmas.

That was rather bad about Vic. It's queer how the people
one thinks would live for ever are the first to go—like Ed
Beanland, for instance. It certainly makes me lonesome to
think of the times only ten years ago. Seems like yesterday,
Ed and Vic and Helen and [Yule ?] and Sallie and us, run-

ning over the streets all night and living in the present—and here we are scattered to the four corners—figuratively. I never dreamed then that the time would come to see Jack in France and me flying in Canada—both of us bent on attending a party that the host him self doesn't even want any more. Still, when its all over and Jack and I are back again and we are sitting around the table at night, we'll go back about ten years and start living there, for even though we are both objective kids now, I can—and Jackie too—realize that home is greater that war, or lightening or marriage or any other unavoidable thing. Isnt it queer that the ones whose home life has been every thing, beginning and ending both, are the ones who go when the time comes, and the ones to whom home is merely a place to eat and sleep— Avents, for instance—do everything possible to go? It isnt so queer, though, for only he whose heart and soul is wrapped about his home can see beyond the utterly worthless but human emotions such as selfishness, and know that home is the thing worth having above every thing, and it is well known that what is not worth fighting for is not worth having. So at Christmas, I hope. If I am sent over at the end of this course, it will be sooner, though now I cannot tell at all.

Billy

I have a fountain pen now, as you have doubtless guessed, having advanced this far through my barrage. Give Dean my love. How is Mammy getting along.

To Mrs. M. C. Faulkner   Thursday [24 Oct. 1918]
[env]   [Toronto]

Dear Mother

I got the tooth paste allright, also three letters and one from Sallie, which I shall answer when I am not feeling so blue. Every thing is going wrong with me. I have been saving money to buy a new tunic with, and yesterday I got a bill that I cant imagine how in the world I ever forgot about, so I am paying it. Then today is pay-day, and they had to call us all out on the parade ground and wasted time until the "F's" were all paid, so I didnt get any thing. And the trouble is, this has happened for the last three weeks. Havent drawn any pay since the first week I was here. I havent needed any yet, but now that I want to send the money for the bill, I couldnt get my $21.00 at all. I have the last three money orders you sent, though—$10, 3, 5—I will cash them as soon as they let us out. I think I'll be paraded to-morrow and get my money, if I can. And on top of all that, I have an awful headache.

But enough of my miseries. I had a letter from Oliver today. Tell him, if you happen to see him, that I am writing him this week. I am going to write you again in the morning, because I shall feel better then.

I am still eating as usual—I mean like a horse. We are learning Aerial Navigation—plotting courses on maps with instruments and compasses and learning theories of flight and "lift" and "drift" and "stagger" and more things than you ever had.

[no signature]

To Mrs. M. C. Falkner   Friday [25 Oct. 1918]
[env]   [Toronto]

Mother darling—

The cake, Hearst's and the Post all came to-day, and I have had a great time today, thinking of the cake, as I havent opened it yet. I am in better spirits to night, $7.00 more at bridge. I'll be a multimillionaire by the time the quarantine lifts.

I heard a funny story today—It was in the medical examining room of an draft exemption board. There were three men at the doctor's desk—a little, undersized Jew, and two Americans. The doctor called up the Yid first—"Well, what exemption do you claim?"

"I dont claim notting's, Doctor. I only want I should be sent right away to France tomorrow. I dont want the Government should spend no money on me training me und buying me a outfit, I only want to go to morrow to the trenches to fight."

The doctor clapped him on the back and told him what a fine patriot he was, and turned to the other two. One of them claimed a bad heart and the other flat feet. "You are a fine pair," he told them, "you, American-born, trying to evade the draft! Just look at this poor Jewish lad, foreign born, who has had none of the priviledges you two have abused all your lives! Look at him, willing to give his life for you two slackers!"

The Jew, in his corner, spoke, insinuatingly—

"But, Doctor, dondt you t'ink I'm a liddle crazy?"

We are going on a 25 mile route march to-morrow. Ye Gods!

            Billy

To Mrs. M. C. Faulkner   Monday [28 Oct. 1918]
[env]   [Toronto]

I had a letter from Katrina today, a nicely typewritten one, from her office. I was glad to hear from her again, for she and Phil and I used to make some wild plans about Phil's office when he became a lawyer, she to be stenog. and me office boy, our job being to sit with our feet on a desk and smoke cigarettes and thus hold all customers spell bound until Phil came to fleece them.

I carry a jar of jelly down to meals with me now. It is very good. And I would certainly be dangerous entrusted with a defenseless fried chicken now. It rained to beat hell today— gee, I didnt mean to write that, but some one just came in the room and remarked that he was hungry as hell and grabbed an apple off of Delaney's—my room mates—bed. It did rain though. We stayed religiously in, despite the frenzied curses of the flight-sergeant, who called us blight- ers and wanted blasphemously to know if we were cowards enough to be "afride of a little rine" We did not go out, though, but ate largely of apples and remained virtuously in

I wish I could raise enough pep to write the letters I should, but I cant seem to. Give Phil my love when you see him. Will write him some day soon, also Sallie.

        Billy

To Mrs. M. C. Falkner   Wednesday [30 Oct. 1918]
[env]   [Toronto]

There are all kinds of rumors going around that quaran- tine is to be lifted today, but I seriously doubt it my self. I am getting to work now, for some of this stuff is rather deep, and examinations begin week after next. And I have no intention of flunking. I wish I could know just when I am to get leave for home, but I cant, so I say Xmas as a modest guess. Sometimes cadets are sent overseas as soon as they complete this course and pass the exams at the S. of A. and are given about 17 days then. If they are not sent overseas, leave depends on the sort of story you put up to the commanding officer. So if I am not sent over, I hope to have completed my training by Xmas, and if so, I'll get some leave then to come home, a brand new lieutenant.

Did the kid get the letter I wrote him?

Billy

To Mrs. M. C. Falkner   Thursday, 31 [Oct. 1918]
[env]   [Toronto]

Momsey dear—

I got your letter yesterday. I am not taking the flu, and have no intention of doing so what ever. In fact, the epidemic is about over here. The churches and theatres open this week, and we come out of quarantine Monday—so they say, but we've been had before about that. Even the children in the Air Force give 'em the merry ha-ha when they say that.

About the tunic, I am not going to get it, I can do without, for we will be given new ones soon, so I am going to invest in a pair of trousers, for I will have to have them, as these are past wearing down town. I am going to make it my self, if possible, but if I cant, I am going to ask for help. This quarantine has been a help rather than a hindrance, for besides the $18.00 I have in money orders, the Paying Officer owes me $16.00. I sent part of the bill last week, and am sending the balance next week. I can tell then how much I will need   Heaven knows I hate to ask for things, as you and Dad have been so sweet to me all my long 21 years.

I didnt intend to give the impression of such abysmal depression as I think you got from my letter—I think you would have known it any way, even if I had not written, I have never been very successful at fooling you, have I?—but I made me feel rather blue to see the money I had saved ever since June go like it did. However, it's done now, and I feel allright about it.

I am going to get the pants as soon as I can go down town again—AND a hair cut. A French Canadian told me the other day—By gar, she's-a long like a bear skin coat, aint she? And I admitted that "she" was. Fact, "she" darn near reaches my waist. I glue her up every morning with cold cream, lest she trip me up.

Wish you could see me taking 15 words a minute at wireless. That's a letter every three seconds.

Love you
Billy

To Mrs. M. C. Falkner   Sunday [3 Nov. 1918]
[env]   [Toronto]

I can always think of lots of things to write when there is no chance of writing, but when I can write I seem never to have anything at all worth saying. Time is certainly moving along any way. First thing you know it will be Xmas and I certainly hope I'll be home by then. There was another church parade this morning. I dont like the Church of England any better than our Protestant, so I think I'll have a shot at the Roman Catholic next   My room-mate, Delaney, is an R.C. Says his prayers very religiously every night.

Please send me Vannye's[1] address when you write. I got the socks and sweater all right. The sweater certainly does fit me snugly. I could just get in it without stretching it all out of shape. It is still getting colder. We will have snow before long and when it snows here it snows. I have got enough knitted things to keep warm, however. And I have enough socks. I dont need any more, but if you do knit any, let 'em be Khaki colored ones.

I'd like to have one pair of Khaki socks, though I dont need any more at all. I wish I could think of what it was I had to say. Something to tell Dad especially, but its gone now, perhaps I'll remember it tomorrow, when I write again.

The kid is becoming a regular Dead-Eye Dick with his gun, killing a squirrel every day. They have a new 'plane at the flying field. It's a perfect beauty, lithe as a greyhound, one seater, with a 110 horse power Clerget rotary motor. Talk about your flying! You can turn it about in its own length, and at a 70 mile clip. Its small and has to go at least 60 m.p.h. to stay in the air. I [FIGURE][2]

It must be great handling one of them and I will certainly be glad when I am put in that squadron. An Curtiss lumbers along like a moving van beside it. Lieutenant-Colonel Bishop[3] is in Canada, as you have probably seen in the papers. His home is in Toronto.

I can easily imagine my self freezing to death up here this winter. There is some talk of moving us all to California. no knowing, though, for there are so many rumors going around.[4]

[no signature]

---

[1]Vance Carter Witt, daughter of Faulkner's great-aunt Willie Medora Falkner Carter.

[2]Line drawing of a one-seater biplane.

[3]The legendary Canadian flying ace W. A. "Billy" Bishop.

[4]The bottom third of this sheet has been torn away.

To Mrs. M. C. Falkner   Tuesday [5 Nov. 1918]
[env]   [Toronto]

Mother darling

This is the last week before examinations, which come Saturday, next week we take up artillery observation. It is a map built to represent the earth at a height of 5000 feet, every thing complete, with tiny electric bulbs to represent shell bursts. We pin point them and send the location— something like this—A 21 G 18 C 8–2—by wireless to the instructor, who replies by a series of white strips of cloth laid upon the floor. It is going to be very interesting, and if you find it interesting, you never have any trouble in passing it. That, though, is the case with every thing here. I have learned to find out how far in a certain direction I can fly with a certain amount of petrol, wind at a certain speed and direction, find what my speed going will be, and returning, and at what time I should arrive.

We have about two more weeks here, and then flying camp for good. I am beginning to feel now that I have accomplished something, learning all the dope that officers have to know, such as King's Orders and Regulations, the Air Force Acts, and such other weighty literature.

The whole squadron went to a very impressive funeral this afternoon. It was a young fellow named Bushell[1] whom I knew very well. He was hurt in a football game the other day, accidentally fell against a brick wall, and died; and was given a military funeral, the same as an officer would have been. It was very unusual for a private soldier to get. There was a cadet firing squad, and the four officers—the squadron commander, the disciplinarian officer, the adjutant and the Commanding Officer. They used a gun caisson, and his coffin was covered with a flag. The officers and the squadron bought enough flowers to cover the whole thing.

I certainly would like to be home. Enough to cut wood. From what you say, Dad will be rivalling Mr Gipson when I get home. Is David Carter still doing business at the old stand? And "Toc" Whitehead? I cant imagine his place without Jack and Van Hiler and Roselle and Mal and eleven niggers of various size and condition back there entertaining David, while Red Frazier gets cigarettes out of the tobacco case.

When you see Joby, tell him I asked about him, and that when I become an officer and have a batman, I'll send for him. All the niggers up here have English accents. ~~This place~~

Toronto is full of staff-officers now. With all sorts of gold and red tabs on the lapels and red hat bands. Very important looking, but are really a sort of glorified batmen— answer phones and make engagements and put off the importunate for the big boss. I saw Colonel Bishop the other day.

Regards to Mammy and love to the kid.

Billy

[1]Durla Bushell, a cadet from India, was one of Faulkner's roommates at Wycliffe College.

To Mrs. M. C. Falkner   Thursday [7 Nov. 1918]
[env]   [Toronto]

Dear Momsey

It looks like the whole thing is over. The whole wing has taken a holiday—took it, not received it—and have all marched down town with the band. It will be quite a while until the air clears enough for me to know exactly where I am as regards leave home.

Saturday [9 Nov. 1918]

We all walked out Thursday, went down town. Gee, but I would have liked being in New York that night! There were parades every where, going right through the lobby of the King Edward hotel, blowing horns and throwing confetti and everything. All the officers in Canada were on hand, lieuts and captains and brass hats galore.

Brigadier-General Hoare[1] spoke to us yesterday and said that if peace were really made, we'd be kept here at least four months afterward. That will not affect Xmas leave, however, so if you think best, you can send me rail road fare so I can have money at once, for leave is given so suddenly, you either get it or you dont, that there is really little time to make any preparations once you get leave. Railroad fare at regular rates would be about $80.00. I have not been able to find how the cent-a-mile will affect soldiers in other than the American uniform. I'll see to that as soon as I can, though. If I can travel that way, fare from New York, without Pullman would be about $20 or $25. There would be no change in Canadian transportation rates, so I will need at least $50.00, fare from here to New York is $22.00. I shall have enough for the incidentals of the trip, but I'd like to be sure of at least fifty. Could easily make it then.

I am going to see if it is possible to draw a draft from here. If not, I could wire and you could send money by telegraph.

Examinations next week, then flying camp.

Love
Billy

[1]General C. G. Hoare was commander of the Royal Air Force in Canada.

To Mrs. M. C. Faulkner   Sunday [10 Nov. 1918]
[env]   [Toronto]

Mother and Dad—

Quarantine is lifted now, officially yesterday afternoon and I went down last night and got my britches. They are very nice looking ones, gray whip cord with light colored strapping on the inside of each knee. In a few days now we get our new uniforms, which is somewhat lucky for me, as I have barely lasted through with this one. I look at my old tunic every day with a feeling akin to reverence, for it has certainly stood by me, all through the Jessie Ketcham and the strenuous Long Branch campaign. We have Exams this week, then comes really practical stuff, flying and machine gunning. No use for the latter, if war is really over.

I hope to have my leave about the time the soldiers start returning. I am certainly glad that I have gotten along as far as I have. Soon now I'll have a pilot's log-book all my own, and a pilot's license for use in civil life. I am going to join the Royal Aero Club which is affiliated with the International Aero Club, so that any where I ever go, I'll be able to find friends and so forth.

We certainly had ~~so~~ a great time the other night. All traffic was tied up, and the King Edward hotel was over run by officers and cadets. It's quite a place, no private soldier nor air mechanic allowed in it, only officers and cadets. The lobby was full of all sorts of generals and majors and staff officers. They let us stay out all night.

Have just written Phil, but had only one envelope, so I cant mail his until tomorrow. Had a letter from Katrina yesterday.

                                          Billy

To Mrs. M. C. Faulkner Wednesday [13 Nov. 1918]
[env] [Toronto]

Dear Mother—

I have just written Vannye, thanking her for the things. I suppose you are not glad the whole show is over? We have gone more or less wild since things happened over there. There are all sorts of rumors going around here, that All Americans are to be discharged, that everything—all instruction ceases Saturday, but I doubt if any thing happens before the first of next month, as they are still watching the Huns in Europe. It would be great if we could all be in New York the day Jack gets home, wouldn't it?

Quarantine is lifted now, we can go and come as we like again. Some one stole my overcoat the other day, and it looks as though I'll have to buy a new one, and pay our cousin George V for the one I lost. I am having my squadron sergeant help me look for it, though, and I hope it'll turn up. Of course we are all glad that the fighting is over, but I am certainly glad it lasted long enough for me to get a pilot's license which I can do quite easily now.

Friday [15 Nov. 1918]

My coat is gone. Couldnt find it any where. I am to be issued with a new one, but I'll have to pay for the one I lost. I will need $30.00, $22 for the coat and $8 for having my teeth filled. I dont want to ask, for I have gotten along so far without having to go begging. I know that you and Dad would be glad to do anything for me, which is the reason I dont want to ask.

I will know next week, I hope, more about my future. There will probably be no more flying in Canada this winter.

Glad I've gotten in what I have. Wont it be good to get home! I dream about it every night, now.

Billy

I will get the pin for you as soon as I can. I am going to look around. I can get you a regular pilot's brevet, if you like—a gold pin like this. [FIGURE][1] I'll look around, however, for I know that the one I like best will please you.

Love
Billy

[1]Line drawing of the pin, a crowned eagle with wings spread. A photograph of Faulkner taken in Oxford following his return from Toronto shows him wearing a similar pilot's brevet on the uniform of an R.A.F. officer.

To Mrs. M. C. Faulkner   Sunday [17 Nov. 1918]
[env]   [Toronto]

Mother Dear

Exams come off tomorrow. Further ahead than that I cant tell. We hear one minute that we are to be mustered out, and next that we spend the winter at flying camp. They are still sending men—ones who have finished and are receiving commissions—over seas, why, I dont know. There is no chance that any of us will go. I hate to think of spending the winter in Canada, however.

I borrowed some civilian clothes and wore them down town Monday. Had a great time, too. Every one thought I was a flying officer in mufti. I am going to bone up on my notes to-night. Most of the cadets in the squadron quit studying when the peace came off, consequently there will be very few of them who pass. I am going to try, though, because I have gotten this far and I would hate to think that

I had wasted the last six months.[1] They might either pass the whole squadron or keep us all back.

There is a fellow here named Rockwell. He was born in Canada, but has lived in Meridian all his life. He knows Jack Sharman and Jeff Hamm[2] and the other Meridian boys, and was in the U.S. air service in Texas with Phil ~~Pidgeon~~ Pidgin and Frank Smythe. Its just like being home again to talk with him. He knows sure enough niggers and comes out every once ~~and~~ with sure enough nigger expressions.

I think he is going back to the South with me as soon as we are discharged. I am going to bone up with him tonight. He has been over all this ground before.

Love
Billy

---

[1] Faulkner passed the examinations with a grade of 70 percent.

[2] Jeff Hamm was the first Mississippi boy to see action in France. In 1919–1920 he was a member of Sigma Alpha Epsilon fraternity with Faulkner at the University of Mississippi.

To Mrs. M. C. Faulkner[1]   Tuesday ⎮19 Nov. 1918]
[env]   [Toronto]

Dear Mother and Dad—

They are calling us up in lots of one hundred and I am expecting to be called any day now. I cant tell just when I will be out and on my way home, yet, though I have decided on my route, gotten train schedules and time tables. I can leave here at noon, reach Buffalo in time to get a train to Cincinnati at 8. A.M., leave Cincinnati at 6 or 7 P.M same day, arrive in Birmingham at 11:30 A.M. following day, get a train to Holly Springs which, provided it is not over two hours late, allows me to catch the south bound train and arrive home at 9 or 10 P.M.

About transportation—We are not discharged, only

given indefinite leave, so we are still in the army and pay our own fare home, and must wear the uniform all the time, but our pay goes on just the same, so I'll be getting paid $1.10 per day for taking a vacation. This is to continue for six months, then we receive full discharges and are civilians again[2] We are not even to get clothing allowances, as near as I can tell, though there are so many conflicting rumors about as to just what is happening.

If we were getting complete discharges now, it would take two or three months before we were all out, as it is, we are called up by name, given a medical examination, and told to beat it away. Gee, when I think about getting home and just doing absolutely nothing but sit, not having to jump in a cold perspiration expecting to hear a whistle blow and some very uneducated voice say—"Double hout 'ere, these men"—or be called at some such hour as four o'clock A.M, made to stand shivering on an aerodrome, waiting for enough light to go up and freeze by. Flying is a great game, but I much prefer walking in the winter. Still, I wouldn't take anything for my little four hours.

I feel lots better, now that I have my transportation safely. I'd hate to be left here without even the army to belong to, not even an address. So I may be home this week and it may be Saturday before I go up, but I am hoping that my name will be among the first drawn. (All names were put in a box and were drawn out one at at time.)

So I'll wire you when I leave Toronto, when I get left by a train, I'll wire also, so you can meet me without trying to catch more than on train to do it.

Cheer-O
Billy

---

[1]Faulkner enclosed with this letter, or one written soon after it, a photograph of the School of Aeronautics squadron from the Toronto *Star-Weekly*, November 17, 1918,

labeled "Toronto Air Cadets Parade * Brothers in Arms." The piece bears a pencilled arrow with the word "ME."

²Faulkner's formal discharge from the R.A.F. is dated January 4, 1919.

To Mrs. M. C. Falkner   Friday [22 Nov. 1918]
[env]   [Toronto]

Mother darling—

We all go up for discharge this morning and as near as I can tell, I'll be on my way home in three weeks, or next week, perhaps. They have told us to make all our preparations to start home, so now all we do is wait for our papers. You can send me some money or I can wire for some, but I dont want to have to wait for it up here after my discharge. I am going to be ready to leave the day we are given discharges. I will need $50.00, about, as I have three weeks back salary coming to me, which I shall get the week before I go, probably. It is so uncertain that I am not taking any chances on having to wait for fare home, am going to make all my preparations beforehand.

I passed my examinations, though it will do me no good, still knowing the I was one of the 20% who ~~failed~~ passed and not one of the 80% who failed, is some thing.

Golly but I am glad to know that at last I am on my way home, for this country is just too cold for any use whatever. I went out last night and nearly froze to death before I could get back. It's snowing out now.

I weighed last night, 132 pounds. More than I ever weighed in my life. When I joined up I weighed 113, if you remember.

I am certainly going to be glad to get home. This weather is awful. I came down the other day, so cold that I had to be lifted out of the machine, could scarcely stand. It is Mississippi for me!

They are going to start demobilization about Monday, so that if every thing moves along as it should, I'll be on my way home in three weeks. I think I'll be given a suit of clothes, civilian clothes, by the Air Force, so I'll be fixed in that particular, at least. I want to have my money all ready in plenty of time, so that I can take the first train south. And Oh, Boy, when I get far enough south to see a few sho nuff niggers!

If I go by New York, I'll probably have time to see Katrina and Mrs Carter, though I am not going to waste any time on my way home. And the next war I go to is going to be in a far, far warmer place than Canada.

The Canadian Expeditionary Force is being demobilized at the same time. I am glad that I am getting out before the soldiers overseas get home. There'll be no living here then, for the flying corps is not very popular in Toronto anyway, because cadets go around in officers uniforms is one reason, then they have a very bad name generally.

Last night I went down town with two other fellows, and passed a bunch of infantry, and they started singing—

> Infantry, cavalry, artillery behind them
> But when you looked for the flying corps,
> Be damned if you could find them

The C.E.F. and the R.A.F. have nice friendly riots every so often.

You can send the money by P.O. money order, cashier's check, or by telegram. And it wont be long till I'm home.

I love you
Billy

To Mrs. M. C. Falkner   Sunday [24 Nov. 1918]
[env]   [Toronto]

Dear Mother and Dad—

They are saying now that we will be out this week, so I am wiring tomorrow for railroad fare home. You dont know how good it makes me feel to know that I'll be on my way home soon, perhaps this coming week. I am rather disappointed in the Royal Flying Corps, that is, in the way they have treated us, however. I have got my four hours solo to show for it, but they wont give us pilot's certificates even. Nothing but discharges as second airmen. It's a shame. Even the chaps who have their commissions and are almost through flying are being discharged the same way. I am too glad to be on my way home at last, to let things like that worry me. They might at least have let me have another hours solo flying, so I could have joined the Royal Aero Club and gotten a pilot's certificate. As it is, I have nothing to show for my six months except my 18 pounds I've gained.

I will write again, as my plans develop further, so I can say exactly the day I am to leave Toronto. They started yesterday calling us up for examination. Our numbers are called, we go down, strip, and are examined by various satellites of the M.O. You pass exams to get in and you pass exams to get out. I hope I'll not have to pass an examination to cross the international boundry. Afraid that I'll be so anxious to get home that I'll ball things up some way.

The jelly and cheese came and was consumed forthwith and immediate, as some justly celebrated portrayer of things Western says in his stories.

Tell Phil when you see him that I am coming home soon, and tell Dean to prepare his gun to kill the fatted calf, unless Pop intends getting one already dead from the University.[1] Most of the people who have been attached to the university in any form or fashion usually manage some of the more important necessaries of life therefrom, such as Ford cars, etc. Tell Pop that if he cant get at least our Xmas dinner out there, that I say he's no good and had no business marrying into our family. Oh, boy, but I mean I'm coming home. I'm Alabama bound, and if I miss the train, I've got a mule to ride!

Love,
Billy

¹Murry Falkner was appointed assistant secretary of the University of Mississippi on December 1, 1918.

To Mr. M. C. Falkner   November 24–25, 1918
[telegram]   8.11 A.M.
                             Toronto

DEAR DAD WE ARE TO BE DISCHARGED WEDNESDAY PLEASE SEND ME SIXTY DOLLARS RAILROAD FARE HOME WILL LET YOU KNOW MY ROUTE HOME AND WHEN TO EXPECT ME AS SOON AS POSSIBLE LOVE TO MOTHER
[t] WILLIAM

To Mrs. M. C. Falkner   Thursday [28 Nov. 1918]
[env]   [Toronto]

Darling Mother—

I am just "marking time" until my papers come through now. I am all packed up, waiting until I can get a train homeward. They are releasing a hundred or so every day, now. I am just waiting until my number is called out.

I have quit sleeping at night now for thinking about getting home. I have so much to tell, things that I was not allowed to write while the war was on, fact, we were not allowed to say any thing at all about flying.

Just now I am trying to find some way of getting all my stuff home. As we are going on leave, not being discharged, we cant turn any of our kit in, but must take it all with us. I've lugged those darn kit bags over all the face of Ontario; now it seems as though I am to carry them all over the states also.

All we do now is lie on our beds until our name is shouted, rather, waiting for them to yell it out. No parades—except mess parades—no drill, no roll calls. We can leave when we like and stay as long as we like. Me, however, takes no chances of having my name called when I am "nappoo." I am all ready, have my money cached away so I can take my foot in my hand. I I wrote Jack on the 15th, hoping he gets it Xmas, or thereabouts.

I love you
Billy

I have your pin. It's very pretty, a good pilot's brevet. I am bringing the kid a cap.

To Mrs. M. C. Falkner   Saturday [30 Nov. 1918]
[env]   [Toronto]

Dear Momsey

It's snowing to beat time here today It's very pretty and all that, but its being dreadfully overdone. There must be at least two inches already, by night we'll be unable to walk for it. Then they'll make us shovel a path from here to Hudson's bay, probably. They have tried everything else.

I am still waiting for my name to be called out. My usual luck, though, seems to be on the job. They are hitting numbers all around me but I am coming through unscathed. There will be no more flying here this winter. They have started dismantling the 'planes and putting them away, a job that has been most magnanimously given to us. So we go down to the hangars, pick up a small washer or strut, or perhaps a wheel, put it down behind the nearest corner and come back to barracks fearlessly, often through a barrage of language from the flight sergeant.

It makes me so darned mad every time I look at my suit case all packed and waiting for my discharge, and seeing all the fellows going, that I feel like going to the adjutant and asking him what is the matter with this army. Just as soon as I get my papers, I'll wire you.

Billy

To Mrs. M. C. Faulkner   Wednesday, 4 [Dec. 1918]
[env]   [Toronto]

Dear Mother—

I was called up today and as near as I can tell, I start home Friday night; provided of course, that things go along as usual and I am not held up by anything. It takes about three days to be examined, and I am expecting to be given all my papers Friday morning.

It's still snowing here, cold as time   The cold doesnt bother me now, however, as I know I am virtually on my way home. Paid for the coat I had stolen, and bought another one from an officer who was hard up, a coat that I can wear when I go into civvies again.

I cant hardly wait to get my papers to start home with. Will wire when I leave.

Billy[1]

---

[1]Below the signature, a penciled note in another hand reads, "And here we leave it to George. Heavens! what wit!"

To Mrs. M. C. Faulkner   December 9, 1918
[telegram]   5 P.M.
           Cinninati, Ohio

LEFT TORONTO YESTERDAY HOME TOMORROW NIGHT OR NEXT DAY
              [t] BILLY

OCTOBER TO
DECEMBER

H-20542

1921

N 1919–1920 Faulkner was briefly enrolled as a special student at the University of Mississippi, where his efforts were more literary than academic. He wrote reviews and poems for the university newspaper, provided illustrations for the annual, and composed the verse play *The Marionettes*, which he hand printed, illustrated, and bound in several copies. Determined to make his way as a writer, he returned to the East in the autumn of 1921, first to New Haven in October and then to New York, where the Mississippi novelist and poet Stark Young had arranged a job for him at the Doubleday bookstore in Lord and Taylor.

The letters from this period are both witty and quite beautiful, and they show Faulkner at age twenty-four self-consciously working to become an imaginative artist. In New Haven, while he waited for Young to summon him to New York, he renewed his friendship with people he had met there in 1918 and settled into a schedule of writing in the mornings, wandering New Haven in the afternoons, often with a sketch pad, and reading and talking with friends in the evenings. The beauty of the New England autumn made a deep impression, and as always the sea held for him a special enchantment. He was writing stories he planned to try on the New York magazines, and he was drawing. At the end of the first week, he sent his mother a page of line drawings of Yale undergraduates and two crayon sketches, the latter unique to his small canon of pictorial work. At the end of the month, he sent Maud Falkner one of several unidentified stories he had submitted for publication. Late in October he worked at odd jobs to replace $20 he had lost, and he joined Stark Young in New York early in November.

In New York he stayed briefly with Young before finding rooms of his own at 655 Lexington Avenue and later at 35 Vandam Street in Greenwich Village. He had been briefly to the city twice in 1918. Now he learned to ride the subways and city buses, visited museums, and talked with other aspiring artists. He planned to supplement his salary by selling his drawings to ad agencies until he could break in with the magazines. On November 14 he went to work at the Doubleday store, where the manager was Young's friend Elizabeth Prall. A month earlier, Major Oldham had written from Mississippi to offer him the job of university postmaster, for which Jack Falkner had been a candidate. Now Oldham renewed that offer, and Faulkner decided to accept. Reluctantly, he brought his second Eastern trip to an end and returned home before Christmas.

To Mrs. M. C. Falkner   Thursday [6 Oct. 1921]
[env]   New Haven

Now, Mother, dont you be downhearted about me at all, as I intend having the time of my life here. I've got a room with three other fellows in a dormitory—only cost $2 a week, and I can live on a dollar a day and another dollar a week for laundry. So I am all right, as I got here with forty dollars. Mr. Stark[1] hasn't come yet, so I left an address at his office in New York so he can tell me when to come down and go to work. I have already found "Smitty" and Al DeLacey[2] got the room for me.

My pass was only good as far as Bristol, that made a hole

in my money, but it's worth money to pass through West Va. and Virginia—red and yellow gum trees, and sudden tortuous rocky streams of clear water; then to slide around the shoulder of a mountain a million miles up in the air, upon the wide reaches of a blue river and little clean towns that look like toys; and the whole thing against a background of blue mountain ranges. We'll have to make that trip together some day.

There's only one sensation to be compared with seeing mountains, and that's seeing the ocean again. Coming up along the sound yesterday I was looking for it all the time; there's a strange feeling in the air: you pass through tight little New England villages built around plots of grass they call greens. The sky toward the sea is pale, about the color of salt, against which the inevitable white church spires are drawn clearer and whiter still. Every where the trees are turning—fall has already come here—ferns, and gum trees, all the underbrush is yellow and red, and over the whole thing is a queer feeling, an awareness of the slow magnificent ocean, like something you have heard or smelled, and forgotten. Then, suddenly, you see it, a blue hill going up and up, beyond the borders of the world, to the salt colored sky, and white whirling necklaces of gulls, and, if you look long enough, a great vague ship solemnly going some where. I cant express how it makes me feel to see it again, there is a feeling of the most utter relief, as if I could close my eyes, knowing that I had found again someone who loved me years and years ago.

New Haven is a nice old place. Auntee[3] would be wild here, all the seniors wear knickers and woolen stockings, and they are allowed to go bareheaded.

This morning I'm going to walk out to East Rock, to have a good look at the sea, and meet Smitty when his school is out.

I havent a permanent address yet, though anything of importance can be sent me care of the Brick Row Book Shop, New Haven. I haven't heard from Mr. Stark, so I dont know if I'll stay here or not. I like New Haven much better than New York.

> Love to everybody,
> Billy

¹Stark Young, Mississippi poet and novelist (1881–1963) then living in New York. Young's best known-book is *So Red the Rose* (1934).

²Friends of Phil Stone's whom Faulkner met in New Haven in 1918. S. B. "Smitty" Smith lived with them then at 120 York Street; he was a principal in the New Haven city schools. DeLacey worked at the Brick Row Book Shop.

³Faulkner's paternal aunt, Mary Holland Wilkins.

To Mrs. M. C. Falkner   Sunday [9 Oct. 1921]
[env]   [New Haven]

Dear Mother—

Cold as cold today. Yesterday morning I walked out to East Rock—get Phil to tell you about it—with some crayons and a sketch block. It was warm, slightly overcast, and about noon it began to rain, a steady autumnal drizzle. The car line, about a half mile away, is visible for about two miles of its length, so I timed myself so as to make a car, and left the summit house and ran for it. Well, of course I missed the car, waited in the rain ten minutes and caught a jitney which carried me within three blocks of home. So by the time I got in, I was soaking. The rain kept up all afternoon, until about six, when Al DeLacey, who lives down on the shore, came along and took me home with him. This morning it was bright and freezing, felt good, though:—the air was crisp and fine, so I walked back today—ten miles— had a bath and rested and read, then about six I went out and had a good meal. I haven't spent anything for food today—Al gave me breakfast—so I spread myself with 75¢ to spend—two pork chops and potatoes and apple pie, all for 55¢.

I am expecting to hear from Mr. Stark within the next few days, then I'll go to New York to stay awhile. I'd much rather live in New Haven, except for the greater number of people in New York with whom to talk.

I'm living in the Divinity School now, in Taylor Hall. Al loaned me bed clothing. If I stay here I shall need two sheets and two blankets. I'll write and tell you what I decide, and if you have them to spare you can send them. I'll be alright with Al's bed clothes until I decide. Love to everybody.

Billy

To Mrs. M. C. Falkner[1]   Thursday [13 Oct. 1921]
[env]   [New Haven]

Dear Mother—

It has turned cold again, but it is clear and crisp—just right for walking. New Haven is beautiful this time of year, especially around the campus, with all the old buildings of gray and white and faded pink stone absorbing sunlight, and all the trees scarlet and flame color. There is a new building—the Joshua Harkness memorial—just finished, an enormous pale yellow Gothic building, with queer windows and minarets and towers that look like lace. The principal tower has windows the panes of which have colored pictures let in the glass someway, and no two of them are alike; and the roof is of hand chipped maroon slate. Its marvelous, I've been trying to draw it, but I haven't got a decent one yet.

I haven't heard from Mr. Stark yet. I think I shall write

him today. I left a note for him at his office, and as I haven't heard yet, I imagine he hasn't come yet, or they lost it. However, I am well enough satisfied here, Al DeLacey lets me read in the Book Shop, and I only spent seven dollars in the last seven days.

I have an idea for a thing, but I'm enjoying myself too much, sitting in the sun watching the ocean, to write it yet. When I go to New York I'm going to take an armful of my things and go from magazine to magazine until I sell 'em.

I saw Rufus Creekmore[2] across the street yesterday. Law school, I imagine.

Love to everybody,
Billy

Oh, yes. Mother, please get a book, Le Jardin d'Epicure, by Anatole France, out of my room and send it to Aunt Bama,[3] 944 Peabody Ave, Memphis. Its a yellow paper back book, in French.

---

[1]Faulkner enclosed with the letter three 8-by-10-inch sheets of drawings. The first, inscribed "A few 'types' They all look like expensively dressed tramps," consists of line drawings in pencil of four male figures drawn variously from front, side, and rear views, the two without hats labeled "seniors." A similar head and torso of a man in hat, coat, and vest is on the verso. The second and third sheets are colored crayon sketches: a seascape titled "From Fort Hale Cliffs across the mouth of New Haven harbor with a heavy sea running," and a landscape titled "RESERVOIR."

[2]Rufus Creekmore was a member of Sigma Alpha Epsilon fraternity with Faulkner at the University of Mississippi. In 1919 he captained the Mississippi football team.

[3]Faulkner's paternal great-aunt, Alabama Leroy Falkner McLean.

To Mr. M. C. Falkner   Monday [17 Oct. 1921]
[env]   [New Haven]

Dear Dad—

I heard from Mr. Stark Saturday, and I think I'll move to New York this week; or as soon as the job is open. I'm going to stay here as long as possible, as I can live cheaper.

Yale has been cleaning up. Beat North Carolina and Williams the last two Saturdays, and Army plays this week. Everyone predicts a good game, for the Yale first team men will play in this game. They have a queer way of coaching here: the crack players, who will play against Princeton and Harvard, dont take part in the earlier games, they dont care whether or not they win them, but are saved for two or three big ones. All West Point is coming up, and are going to drill in the Bowl before the game.

Well, sir, I could live in this country a hundred years and never get used to the niggers. The whites and niggers are always antagonistic, hate each other, and yet go to the same shows and smaller restaurants, and call each other by first names. I was standing in front of the Yale Post Office yesterday, beside a nice looking well dressed fellow, when two dressed up nigger boys came along. One of the niggers said Well, laddo, how's the boy? The white fellow said—Fine, Paul, fine. And the nigger said—Say, Ed, call me up to night; got a party on. And they kidded each other like that for about five minutes. You cant tell me these niggers are as happy and contented as ours are, all this freedom does is to make them miserable because they are not white, so that they hate the white people more than ever, and the whites are afraid of them. There's only one sensible way to treat them, like we treat Brad Farmer and Calvin and Uncle George.

Everybody all right? I had a letter from Mother Friday.

Love
Billy

To Mrs. M. C. Falkner   Thursday [20 Oct. 1921]
[env]   [New Haven]

Dear Mother—

I swapped my old light weight suit for a fleece lining for my trench coat, the lining, however, has no sleeves in it; so will you please make me a pair of sleeves from an old blanket or some heavy cloth? Just rough sleeves, the shoulder ends about 22 inches around the armpit, that is, 11 inches measured across flattened out. It's a dandy skin, thoroughly wind proof, almost the length of the entire coat. A heavy blanket will do the trick, or sleeves from an old mackinaw if we have one. You can put them in the suit case with my blue suit, also a big needle and thread, and I can sew them in myself. I dont need the other suit yet, my plans are still hanging fire, and I had rather have the suit case sent to New York than sent here for me to lug down there.

This beautiful indian summer is over at last, it started raining this morning, a cold drizzle, wind from the north. It has certainly been lovely while it lasted, though,—the hills all misted over with azure and gold, grey stone fences half covered by copses of flame colored berry bushes, round yellow pumpkins in fields of shocked corn, and maple forests, yellow and red beside soft blue water, and all against sombre black pines and purple hills. And at night, with the harvest moon making everything vague and silver and silent, as though waiting for some spirit of the woods and fields to come forth and solemnly gesture against the moon.

I have recovered my dog again, and have written several things; I have one that is worth money at anytime, same as a commercial paper or a banker's note. I'll hold on to it though, for a while, anyway.

Al DeLacey had a letter from Phil wanting to know why in hell I hadn't written him. If you see Phil, tell him I have written him, and if he wants to help the cause, to send me a can of tobacco.

There's a big football game Saturday—Army vs. Yale. There is a game every Saturday,—Yale doesn't condescend to make trips—and the Freshman team plays someone every Sunday afternoon. They have pretty fair games, too.

Love to every body, and a million for you.

Billy.

To Mrs. W. C. Falkner   Tuesday [25 Oct. 1921]
[env]   [New Haven]

Dear Mother—

You are beginning to think I've forgotten your address, haven't you? I've just finished five days work on a short story which I shall send off tomorrow, and I haven't done another thing except work at it, even though my intentions to write home were praiseworthily vigorous. It's nippy but not unpleasant, they have perfect weather here, it only rains in the fall about once a month, so my walking has not been interfered with. The trees are nearly all bare now, but the air is clear—you can see a thousand miles. For the last month it has been hazy, beautiful, but not very far to see. Now, though, the atmosphere is clear. Sunday I went out to Fort Hale Park and you could see across the sound to Long Island, could see the houses, even, twenty five miles away, as if it was just across the street.

One funny thing: the nights are warm. During the day the north west winds have quite an edge, but they die down at sunset, and the air from the water, which is about fifteen

degrees warmer than the land, b̶l̶ drifts in and it feels like
another part of the country. A friend of Smitty's—Mr
Lyons—had us to dinner at his home Sunday. I enjoyed it
very much, the change from the desiccated grub of the one
arm joints where I do my foraging.

No news at all. I have all the new books I can possibly
read, and a few people with whom to talk occasionally, but
no one as yet whose society I prefer to my own. In fact, I
write in the morning, walk in the afternoon and later watch
the lights go up, then come back here and read at night. I
hope I can sell this story right off, if I can, I'll have a start so
I can continue to live as it jolly well suits me.

I gathered from your last letter that you will have sent the
suit and overcoat by the time you get this. I hope you got
my request for sleeve linings in time.

Oh, yes. I have already stopped traffic in the streets;
fame, in fact, has lighted early upon my furrowed brow. The
other day I was crossing the busy corner in town, at my
usual gait and failed to see the traffic cop turn his stop sign.
I was thinking of something, at lest I guess I was thinking,
of something, anyhow; nevertheless I didn't hear his whistle
at all. So I came to as a car fender brushed the skirts of my
coat and another car appeared so close to me that I couldnt
see my own feet, beside a trolley that stopped resting against
my hat brim. Well, I was the center of excitement, however,
I did manage to climb on the fender of one of the cars while
both chauffeurs and the motor man reviewed my past, present and future, liabilities, assets and aspirations in the most
fluent Americanese. Well, by that time the cop got there, he
bawled out all four of us, while the chauffeurs loudly called
heaven to witness my thorough imbecility. They finally out-
talked the cop and he turned on me, as though I had
snatched a penny from the hand of his yellow haired baby

daughter. "Yes," he shouted, "It was you, all right that balled the whole thing up, I seen you, drooping along. What in the hell do you think you are, anyway—a parade?"

No very cutting reply occuring to me until much later, I made no rejoinder. How ever, I am more careful.

Please get from my dresser drawer a tin box of United Cigar store coupons, and send the coupons to me. I can get shaving soap and tooth paste and razor blades with them.

Dear Dean.[1]

Yes, I saw Yale play West Point. The cadets marched out to the Bowl, with bands and flags, and before the game they drilled on the field. And you should have seen their cheer leader. He danced and turned hand springs and everything. And one trick they had: they would take a boy from the top row of their seats, and roll him like a log over their heads down the grandstand to the bottom row of seats, then roll him back, passing him just like a log from hand to hand above their heads. It was a dandy game, Yale won 14–7. The Army fullback, French is said to be the best football player in this part of the country since that nigger named Pollard who played for Brown some years ago. Next Saturday is the Brown game. I shant go though, but shall save my money for the Princeton game.

Write and tell me about Greenwood.

Billy

[1]Faulkner's youngest brother, Dean Swift Falkner.

To Mrs. M. C. Falkner   Saturday [29 Oct. 1921]
[env]   [New Haven]

Bless you, mother. You've got me so loaded down that I'll
never be able to move at all now. And you bought the cheese
and jam and candy with your own money, didnt you now? I
know you did, though, whatever you say about it. I am sorry
you sent me the good overcoat in place of the old blue one,
for I might be tempted to sell it when I am hard up. I
expect, when I move to New York, I shall send it back. I'll
have too much for any one man to carry at one time, and I'd
hate to sell it for a few dollars.

I sent a story off yesterday, and shall send some more
things—one of which I am enclosing—in a day or so.

Love
Billy

To Mrs. M. C. Falkner   [postmarked 1 Nov. 1921]
[env]   [New Haven]

There was something rather puzzling came up yesterday.
Perhaps you can straighten it out. You mentioned in several
letters that Major Oldham[1] was trying to have Jack appointed Post Master at the University. Well, yesterday I had
a wire from Major asking me if I wanted the job, and saying
he must have an answer immediately. I wired him that I
didn't want it, remembering also what you had written in
regard to Jack and the job. I thought of course, that the
Major had merely offered me the chance before recommend-
ing Jack for it, and I didnt want to spoil Jack's chance, as
well as not wanting the place at all for myself, being thoroughly satisfied here. Then, about a half hour after the
Major's wire, Al DeLacey got one from Phil asking him to

make sure that I got mine, and an hour later I got one from Phil saying take the job. I didn't know what to think then, but supposed that Phil had discussed it with you all and that Jack, for some reason, was not eligible for the place. So I wired the Major again that I would take it.[2] Please look in to this. If the Major couldnt get it for Jack and can for me, all right; but if he's trying to put something over on Jack, get hold of Phil and straighten it out. I hate to think of leaving the east after taking three years to get here, but 1800 a year is too good to let Van Hiler have.

Be sure, mother, and see about the business. That would fix Jack fine if he's fed up with law.

Billy

[1]Oxford attorney, and later judge, Lemuel E. Oldham, Estelle Oldham Franklin's father and Faulkner's future father-in-law.

[2]Faulkner formally accepted the job on November 15, 1921, took the examination for fourth-class postmaster December 10, and served as temporary postmaster until he was confirmed by Senator Pat Harrison in May 1922. He served until he resigned October 31, 1924.

To Mrs. M. C. Falkner   [postmarked 10 Nov. 1921]
[env]   New York City

Poor but Plucky, or
The Wabblings of Will
I (New Haven)

It's all over (for a while) now, and I can tell you about it. I can appreciate the humor myself at present, though I couldnt a week ago. To begin with. About three weeks ago I lost my money. Right out of my pocket, like you said I was going to, leaving me with $2.68 out of my remaining $22.68. I finally had to eat, so I washed dishes in a Greek restaurant, a "one arm" place, for my meals, saving my money for tobacco as long as possible, but finally it gave out and I was out of tobacco for four days. I didnt break my gold piece nor cash your first check, for I wanted them in reserve. ~~After about ten days of this~~ The other dishwashers, Greeks and one Irish, thought I was a wop, and looked down on me.

After about ten days of this I got a job at a Catholic orphanage, raking leaves, washing windows and tending the furnace. I thought at first that I was to wash and feed the orphans, but it evolved otherwise. This job lasted a week, while the present incumbent had a vacation, for food and washing and lodging and $14.00. On the day they paid me off I ~~received~~ returned to town and got your letter of good tidings; and, with my liabilities augmented to $24.00, I came to New York.

CHAPTER II (NEW YORK)

New York is a large town on the west coast of the Atlantic ocean, and is connected to America by the Brooklyn bridge and the 14th street ferry so that as many people as possible from New Jersey and Des Moines Iowa can get here at the same time. Southern exposure and pleasant hours.

Mr Stark lives in Greenwich village, a lovely basement room[1] where you can be lulled to sleep by the passing of the subway trains. I stayed with him last night and spent today looking for a room of my own. Saw two: one, a dreadful place with a wood stove and kerosene lamp, romantically situated in McDougall's alley, and one, very nice, on 7th Ave. not far from Washington Square. I'll take it if I can get it. Rather difficult to get a decent room for less than $15 a week here, as all Oshkosh is here with portfolios of strange verse and stranger pictures under one arm, a Windsor tie, a fountain pen and a cigarette in the other hand, and a pocket full of condensed bouillion cubes, and no razor at all. That is, the males dont seem to have razors. The women all do, I believe.

I shall perhaps start to work Monday, in Lord and Taylor's book shop. Tell every body it's Lord and Taylor's on 5th Ave. A pale oversized replica of an Italian cathedral. Miss Prall, the manager of the book department was very nice to me, gave me dinner last night, and smoked very gracefully while I discussed Art to her. She is a thin, slightly worn youngish woman, smudges under the eyes, and bobbed hair.

Horn rimmed glasses, bobbed hair, and smocks [sic]! Never saw the like in my life. Styles are queer: in Africa they wear their bone rings in the nose instead of the eyes. I shall like it here; Miss Prall tells me I can sell some drawings with out much trouble. I have, also, met an honest-to-God poet, not a Greenwich villager, but a real man: Edwin Arlington Robinson.[2] I was in a book shop up town when he came in, a slender man with a thin gentle face and glasses, and an almost indistinguishable suggestion of indecision in his manner, which may be due to near sightedness. He is forty, I should say, with black hair and moustache. He came in and glanced at me, and I recognized him from his pictures. As he went out he looked at me again—he had come in to autograph his new book—so I went up and spoke to him. Of course, I didn't gain anything from him, as I probably startled him, but he was too gentle to put me off abruptly.

That's about all, except I made my first subway trip yesterday. The experience showed me that we are not descended from monkeys, as some say, but from lice. I never saw anything like it. Great crowds of people cramming underground, and pretty soon here comes a train, and I swear I believe the things are going a mile a minute when they stop.

Well, everybody crowds on, the guards bawling and shoving, then off again, top speed. Its like being shot through a long piece of garden hose.

Subways, surface cars, elevated trains, and taxicabs making walking a snare and a delusion. All the time, day and night, and where in the world they are all going, and so darned, darned fast, I cant imagine. I dont think they know themselves. It's grab your hat and get on, then get off and run a block and get on again.

I'll see some shows next week, perhaps.

Love
Billy

[1]Young rented rooms from Elizabeth Prall, manager of the Doubleday bookstore located in Lord & Taylor. In 1924 she married Sherwood Anderson and moved with him to New Orleans, where Faulkner met her again in 1925.

[2]Faulkner praised the New England poet (1869–1935) in his 1925 essay "Verse Old and Nascent: A Pilgrimage." Robinson's *Collected Poems* was published in 1921.

To Mrs. M. C. Falkner [postmarked 12 Nov. 1921]
[env] [New York]

Dear Mother—

I am settled at last—that is, temporarily—in a garret, hall bedroom, 4 flights (I wonder why they ever called 'em flights?) up. It will do until I find a place I like better, though. I dont care for this especially because it is way up town, close to Central Park and those big insolent apartment houses where all the wealthy people from Texas and St Louis live. I want a place down toward Greenwich village where Mr. Stark lives, but rents are cheaper in this part of town—dont get the impression that I live in one of the afore mentioned apartments. Mine is a snug decayed aristocrat of a brick house, Victorian furniture—red plush and chased imitation pearl insets. Rent $5 per week. The lower part of town is so crowded that you cant get anything near Greenwich village for less than $10. However, I may be able to find something later. My address now is: 655 Lexington Avenue.

I'm having a fine time, and I start to work Monday at Lord and Taylor's bookshop. I've been to the Metropolitan Museum, saw some priceless statues and paintings, some marvelous water colors by Cezanne and some of the Americans, and tomorrow I'm going to Brooklyn to an exhibition of water colors. I have met several embryonic Michaelangelo's in fact, the Museum is crowded with them every afternoon, members of the different Beaux Arts schools go there in coveys to copy pictures of dead fish, and baskets of fruit, and colored parrots. It's terrible, the way they mix pictures there, without any regard for proximity, or lighting, or any thing. A girl I met at a tea party this afternoon is going to arrange for me to join a night drawing class. I want to learn something about line, as you know, ~~I have next~~ to no all my ideas on the subject of line drawing are purely personal. I shall try to augment my income drawing, ads and so forth, while I get on my feet writing.

This town is certainly a wonderful place to be as unpleasant. It's too darned crowded for me ever to like it, but as for possessing means of going from one place to another in a hurry, there's nothing to compare with it. I live about ten miles from Mr Stark, yet I can nip down a hole in the ground, take a subway to the Grand Central [STAIN][1] Terminal, take a shuttle train from there without ever seeing day light, go to Times Square and—still without coming into the world, take another train and pop up out of a hole at Mr Stark's door, all for a nickle. It's marvelous, but you're just like a rat. The best fun, though, is to take a 5th Ave. bus at Washington Square and ride on top of it with the poets and country people up to the end of the avenue, along Riverside drive, then back again to the arch. That's the whole length of Manhattan Island and back, but very expensive: costs 20¢.

This was Armistice day, parades and bands all day. This afternoon Miss Prall, my boss, had a tea party at her apartment, and then asked me to stay for supper. She's very nice.

[no signature]

[1]Next to the stain on the stationery is written, "I dont know what this is, but I cant write on it."

To Mrs. M. C. Falkner   [postmarked 16 Nov. 1921]
[env]   [New York]

Dear Mother:

Dont send any mail to me at the Lexington ave. address at all after you get this letter, as I am moving as soon as possible. This is a rotten place, I overlooked the fact, for two days, that there was no heat in the room, and there are any number of small reasons why my bed is impossible. I wrote—and wired Major yesterday, in receipt of a letter from him saying that he had already sent my name in, that I would take job. He mentioned the fact that Jack would be an assistant. If Major continues to stew over it, just tell him to go ahead and disregard me in the matter. He said, though, that Evern Jones[1] was a stronger local hope than Jack. In that case we'd better keep it in the family, I guess. But for heaven's sake, do something down there about it, instead of continuing to ask me what to do. I dont care one way or the other. Symphony concert next week.

Billy

[1]Lieutenant Evern Jones, of Greene County, Mississippi, was a family friend and political supporter of Senator Pat Harrison. Harrison originally favored Jones, but at

Oldham and Stone's urging, he put forward Faulkner's name, despite Jones's having scored higher on the postal examination.

To Mr. Dean Falkner Sunday [20 Nov. 1921]
[env] [New York]

Dear Sweetness:—

Write to Billy and tell him the names of some books you'd like Xmas. In the store where I work they have the "Connie Morgan" in a book from The Boy's Life Magazine, and some baseball stories written by Christy Matthewson, Indian and Scout and football stories of all kinds; also, tell Mother, the later "Wildcat" stories, and the later "Red Gap" stories. In fact, any book you see advertised at all, we have got it. So write me before the ~~D~~ 10th of December and tell me what you want.

My address now is:
35 Vandam St.

I'm getting along fine, but I miss the 'possum and bird hunting a lot. Still, if Major Oldham gives me the Post Office job, I'll come home after Xmas.

I walked all day today, across the Hudson River in New Jersey, and helped a man fly his aeroplane.

Love to everybody
Billy

Tell mother I got some clothes, sox and shirts, and I dont need any money from home at all.

35 Vandam St New York City.

To Mrs. M. C. Falkner [postmarked 23 Nov. 1921]
[env] [New York]

Dear Moms:

Let me drop a suggestion in all friendliness: dont send any more mail to the store. A place as big as it is cant bother with its retainers' letters as the Brick Row could; in fact, I am reminded of this state of affairs by the floor manager with increasing emphasis each time. They wont even let the help use the telephones. Can you beat that in this democratic country? It's all right so far, that is if they dont fire me when the box comes.

I got Wendell Perry's card. We saw each other in a subway station after I had gotten on the train and they had locked the door. I couldn't get out, and he couldnt get in. I got in communication with him today.

1. Yes, I got the sleeve linings, but saw no dollar bill. However, I will stop and look for it now. Yes, I found it. It had, naturally, never occured to me to open the envelope. For heaven's sake, dont think I feel neglected. I take yours and my love for granted so much that I never worry about it at all. Cheer up! That's the first trace of exasperation I ever saw in your letters.

I do not need any money. If I cant get along on what I make, I shall go to farming next year. I have so far, bought three shirts, three pairs of socks, paid one dollar for laundry since September (wash most of it myself), paid three dollars to have my shoes resoled and one fifty to have my old blue coat dyed—it was faded so. The pants were unfaithful to me, on both sides. Threw them away, as I couldnt sell 'em at any price.

I am now living at 35 Vandam Street, in the village. Rent 3.50 per week and I buy my own fuel. I know I shant move again before the first of December, so address me 35 Vandam st.

I certainly wish I could find a place where they have decent coffee in the morning. I honestly believe the stuff they sell is the water they wash the cups in the night before. I drink coffee only once a day, and smoke only three times. Pretty good, what?

I have your last ll [sic] favor which I shall keep for eventualities. Let me know if you want any books, as I get a 10% discount. I shall buy some for myself soon. They have anything from Zane Grey, Porter and the Henty books[1] to Shakespeare and the Bible.

Billy

[1]The American writer of Westerns Zane Grey was a favorite of Murry Falkner's. Porter may be the English romance novelist Jane Porter (1776–1850), whose *Thaddeus of Warsaw* (1803) was in Faulkner's library at Rowan Oak, or perhaps the American short story writer William Sydney Porter (1862–1910), who wrote under the pen name O. Henry. The Englishman G. A. Henty wrote war stories for boys. His *With Lee in Virginia: A Story of the American Civil War* was in Faulkner's library at Rowan Oak.

JANUARY TO JULY

1925

T HE importance for Faulkner of his six-month residence in New Orleans in 1925 can hardly be exaggerated. It is documented in his life and in his art, and it is substantiated in the forty-two letters he wrote to his mother from New Orleans and the Gulf Coast from January to July. The community of artists and intellectuals in the Vieux Carre were to him in 1925 what he had hoped and imagined Greenwich Village would be when he went to New York four years earlier. The comparison of the two experiences is inescapable, even to the important presence in both places of Elizabeth Prall, now Mrs. Sherwood Anderson, and it is made still more pointed by the undercurrent of cultural competition that existed then between the Eastern United States and the Deep South. What H. L. Mencken had characterized as the arid "Bozart of the South" Sherwood Anderson was praising as the center of the "Modern Movement" in American writing. In New York in 1921, Stark Young's assistance to the young writer had resulted in Faulkner's finding work in the bookshop Elizabeth Prall managed. In New Orleans in 1925, Elizabeth Prall Anderson gave him personal assistance in the form of food and lodging in her home, supported his writing, and encouraged his relationship with her husband, whose artistic stature and literary reputation put him in a position to be of significant help to a young writer.

To the twenty-four-year-old Faulkner, New York had

been a fascinatingly new place and a dizzying adventure, but his letters from New York City in 1921 say nothing of writing. The Southern city proved itself at once more comfortably familiar and more hospitable to his ambitions. Faulkner came to New Orleans in January 1925 a published poet whose work had appeared nationally in the *New Republic* and the New Orleans *Double Dealer* as well as in the university newspaper, *The Mississippian*. In December 1924, with Phil Stone as underwriter, the Four Seas Co. published his first book, the verse eclogues of *The Marble Faun*. Thanks to Stone, the imminent arrival in New Orleans of the "Mississippi Poet" was announced before Christmas in the *Times-Picayune*. In 1921 Faulkner had left the East for home after six weeks. Now, in New Orleans, he postponed his planned European trip and stayed on. Within a month he had sold to the *Times-Picayune* the first in a series of sixteen New Orleans sketches that would run intermittently through September and had placed a poem, an essay, and a sequence of prose vignettes with the *Double Dealer* for January-February, the latter piece for money. The *Double Dealer* for April included still more of his work, and that month the Dallas *Morning News* carried his essay-review of Sherwood Anderson's work.

By the time Anderson returned to the city from a speaking tour early in March, Faulkner had begun work on a novel based in part on his real and imagined experiences in the R.A.F. seven years before. Within a week he reported that he and Anderson were writing a book together; within the month he claimed that he was the inspiration for two Anderson stories and some of the events in Anderson's *Tar: A Midwestern Childhood*. Seen retrospectively through the letters, it is clear that there were other friends in New Orleans important to Faulkner, both men and women. But only Anderson was important enough to require exorcism by satire. At the height of his discipleship, in his April review, Faulkner attributed an experience of their tall-tale character Al Jackson to Anderson himself and characterized Anderson ironically as "A field of corn with a story to tell and a tongue to tell it with." The following year, with Bill Spratling, he would parody his style in *Sherwood Anderson & Other Famous Creoles*.

Unlike these pieces, Faulkner's New Orleans letters admit his real regard and display the extent of his debt to his generous friend. They trace the course of that friendship as they do also the progress of Faulkner's writing. Among other points of critical debate, they make clear that Anderson and his wife did read *Soldiers' Pay*, at various stages of its development, and warmly encouraged Faulkner in it. It was Anderson, in June 1925, who recommended the book to his new publisher, Horace Liveright, and Liveright published it the following year. Faulkner came to New Orleans a poet; he left for Europe in July 1925 a soon-to-be- published novelist. In the interim he demonstrated to his own satisfaction not only that he could live by his writing but that writing was his life.

To Mrs. M. C. Falkner   6 Jan. [1925]
                                            The Lafayette Hotel
                                            New Orleans

Dear Mother—

Phil brought the message. I was so glad to hear from you; I was worried a little, your face looked so white and despairing. So I am so *darned* glad you and pop are willing for me to make the trip,[1] even though you think it foolish. About coming home—I know a better plan than that—you come down here. I will have got settled in a week, and you can plow around for a day or so, and have a grand time. Write me when you can come, and I'll find out about trains.

Now dont say you cant. I am *not* going to cash your check, so you already have $25.00 to make the trip on. Let this year be your Sabbatical—you owe yourself a trip, and probably pop and Dean will get along better without you to nag 'em for a day or so.

Dont write me here.[2] I will have permanent address tomorrow, which I'll send you at once.

My love to every one.
Billy

6 January 1924[3]

[1]Faulkner arrived in New Orleans on January 4, 1925, planning to book passage on a boat for England.

[2]The Lafayette Hotel, where Faulkner and Stone stayed briefly until Faulkner moved to a room in Sherwood and Elizabeth Anderson's apartment at 540 B St. Peter Street in Jackson Square.

[3]Faulkner apparently misdated the letter, writing 1924 for 1925 at the beginning of the new year.

To Mrs. M. C. Falkner   [early Jan. 1925]
                                              [New Orleans]

Dear Mother—

My address is 540 B. St Peter st., with Mrs Anderson. Elizabeth just took me in and gave me a room regardless.

Phil is going by to see you—we've had so much fun I can hardly remember it even to write it down, he'll tell you about whom we have seen, and how dog-gone much we et, and what we have done, and so on.

There are two British cruisers lying in the river—the Calcutta and the Capetown, Vice Admiral Sir J. Ferguson, K.C.M.G., C.B., and New Orleans is filled with boiled sailors. I saw one yesterday who could hardly walk, and their pants flapping makes them look funnier than ever. Well, he looked at me very intently, and said—"God save the Irish." I rejoined with "God save King George," and he said "To hell with King George. My name is Cavanaugh." And I suspect so.

About getting a boat—it is simply a question of being on hand. I dont know when it will be—I am to call at the British Consulate every day until one is available. So it might be just anytime.[1]

I spent the afternoon aboard the "Calcutta," and had a good time. It's an oil burner, about 300 feet long, with four 6 inch guns and four torpedo tubes and two anti aircraft ~~batteri~~ guns, all steel, and litle narrow steel gangways, and 408 officers and men. I dont see where in the world they put them, nor what they do.

Is Jimmy[2] getting any fatter than his usual health? Wish I could see the rascal.

Billy

[1]Ultimately, Faulkner would delay his European trip six months. He sailed for Europe aboard the *West Ivis* July 7, 1925.

[2]Faulkner's nephew, John Falkner's son James Murry Falkner, born on July 18, 1918.

To Mrs. M. C. Falkner   Monday
                            [probably 12 Jan. 1925]
                            [New Orleans]

Dear Mother, do you remember Harry Rainold[1]—a biggish
sort of a boy I liked while we were in school in 1920 or 21? I
met him on the street the other day, and I spent the week
end at his home in Pass Christian. This place is the Newport
of the Gulf Coast, all rich folks. The Rainolds have a big one
story sprawling house facing the gulf—a nice house, with
wood fire places and a bath for every room. We got there
Saturday evening in time for dinner. They are grand people,
they let you do whatever you want to—dont try to entertain
you, you know. Dr Rainold is a funny light little man, and
Mrs Rainold is like Mrs Eatman. They were sitting before
the fire reading, and spoke to us, and then went on reading.
I never have felt as completely at home. They didnt try to
"talk" to me at all, let me get a book and read too. We went
to bed early, got up the next morning at 7:30 and went horse
back riding until 9, came in for breakfast, then went down
to Gulfport and played golf until four, came back for dinner, sat around and talked, had tea about 7, then to bed.
Nice and quiet. I enjoyed the gulf, just looking at it. Harry
and I went out to the end of the pier Saturday night, and
rode along the beach Sunday morning, and I walked about
two miles along it last evening at sunset, watching the fishing boats coming in, and the gulls wheeling, and the spars of
schooners and the long piers black as ink against the west.
They have no bare trees here at all. The live oaks are thick
and green, and palms everywhere. And grass! never in my
life saw I such green grass. It looks like it might be poison—
as though a cow would take one bite, and drop like a shot,
like in the Swede's place in Red Gap.[2] The gulf coast is
certainly the place for you and pop to move to. Last night

was a cold day here, people in overcoats, and I played golf in my shirt sleeves. I wonder what they consider a really warm day. I have but two objections to it—it is liable to rain any time, and the oyster shells smell so bad.

I wrote you about those two British cruisers which were here, didnt I? They dropped down the river Saturday. When they passed the two American warships they dropped their flags, and both vessels were signalling each other with flags, and the American ships playing "The Star Spangled Banner," and the British cruisers "God Save the King." Every time a foreign vessel passes the warships the flag is dipped. The warships very haughtily do not reply.

Mrs Anderson has taken me in to live with them. She is so nice to me—mothers me, and looks after me, and gets things to eat which I like.

Give every one my love.

Billy

Monday.

540 B S̶t̶.̶ ̶P̶e̶t̶e̶r̶ St
Saint Peter St.

There are two Peter Sts here.

---

[1]Harold "Dutch" Rainold was a member of Sigma Alpha Epsilon fraternity with Faulkner at the University of Mississippi, 1919–1920.

[2]In Harry Leon Wilson's humorous novel *Ruggles of Red Gap* (1915).

To   Mrs.   M.   C.   Falkner   [mid-Jan. 1925]
                                          [New Orleans]

Dear Mother—

The candy came today, and went, practically—between Bob[1] and me. Did Phil tell you about Bob? He's a fine boy.

Mrs Anderson treats us both just alike, sees that we have enough to eat, and enough cover, and takes care of our money for us.

Bob and I get up at 7, cook our own breakfast, I spend the forenoons writing, and the afternoons plowing about, meeting strange people. I am writing a series of short sketches (stories) which I am trying to sell to a newspaper. Took one to the editor of the Times-Picayune yesterday.[2] He said he didnt have time to read it, and told me to leave it and call in a day or two; then he glanced at the title, read the first sentence, then the first page, then the whole thing with a half finished letter in his typewriter and three reporters waiting to speak to him. He was tickled to death with it, and has put it before his board. I have just finished another one which I shall take him tomorrow. If he wont take them, I will try the other big paper, the Item. Bob Anderson works on it, and he has been telling them about me.

If they take them, it means 5.00 per column. So I can earn at least 5.00 any day I feel like writing. Hope they do. I will be sure to send you the paper, in case.

Bob and I have toast and coffee and marmalade and grape fruit for breakfast; I eat no lunch and buy a good meal at night. At the French and Italian lower class restaurants you get a whale of a dinner for seventy five cents. So I can live on a dollar a day easily. Cheaper if necessary. Harry Rainold got me a card to a Gymnasium Club, with a swimming pool and everything. Grand.

Billy

Please send my thin Raincoat

---

[1] Robert Lane Anderson (b. 1907), Sherwood Anderson's eldest son.

[2] Either John McClure, who also was associated with the New Orleans literary magazine the *Double Dealer*, or managing editor Colonel James Edmonds, both of whom Faulkner mentions later. The first of the sixteen sketches subsequently published in

the *Times-Picayune* appeared in McClure's Sunday feature section, February 8, 1925, titled "Mirrors of Chartres Street."

To Mrs. M. C. Falkner   [mid-Jan. 1925]
                                           [New Orleans]

Dear Mother—

The Times-Picayune took those things, and the editor wants all I can do like them. He offered me a column, to do every day—verse and sketches, anything I want to put in it. But that would be too terrible; I prefer writing these stories as I feel like it, rather than have five hundred words to do every day, rain or shine or hell or high water. I will send you the paper whenever they appear. I dont know what he will pay a piece for them yet. At least five dollars per each.

The laundry and the coat came. Thank you. I am all right, having a good time. As I write one of these sketches every day, I feel completely "wrote out" by night, so I shall send you the articles themselves, an as they are all experiences I've had here.

Love to every one, and my kindest personal regards to Dr. Lott and tell him damn his black hide, to sell those clothes. Might see if Miss Lawhon is tired of "standing" for those pants. Hope the purchaser is still standing, or they'll be worn out.

Captain:[1] if you're talking about my paying you or anyone 60¢ under present circumstances, you sho' got de wrong man. Otherwise, kind reverence and gratitude for long friendship.

                                           Billy

[1]Faulkner's youngest brother, Dean Swift Falkner, called Captain for his athletic prowess.

To Mrs. M. C. Falkner   Thursday [22 Jan. 1925]
[env]   [New Orleans]

I seem to be a dreadful correspondent. I write you and say to myself—Now, that's a fine letter: I haven't left out a thing.

Yes, I got the raincoat. Yes, I got the three dollars of antique money. No, I haven't got the check yet.

I am writing some things for a newspaper here. I'll send you them as they appear.

This place is FILLED with beggars, people following the races, you know. All kinds of stories. One lad about fifteen beat his way down here from St Louis, got into jail immediately. He asked me for a nickle and I took him to a restaurant and bought him a real meal. He seemed to be a sweet young chap; told me about his mother and about his trip, and everything. I thought to myself—This might have been the captain, and I filled him up. I get the ideas for the newspaper stories from the beggars I talk to. All sizes and sexes and shapes and conditions (alcoholic) you can imagine.

Everyone here is grand to me—painters and writers, etc. A young painter is calling formally upon me to morrow, and Sunday I am to dine with one of the literary arbiters of New Orleans. Last night I had dinner with John McClure, a poet and literary editor of the Times-Picayune—by the way, he has reviewed my book, next Sunday it will appear, I suppose[1]—and we talked and sipped hot whiskey punch until daylight, then walked down to the river to see the sun rise.

Miss Elizabeth sees that I eat enough, askes me every day if I remembered to get lunch. I spend all the forenoon writing, and in the afternoon I walk about and talk to all the bums and cops and strange people, and in the evening we gather somewhere and discuss the world and politics and art and death, etc.

I have borrowed golf clubs from Harry Rainold and Sundays Bob Anderson and Harold Levy[2], a musician, and I play golf at City Park—50¢ for all day.

So I am getting along fine. If you ~~folks~~ and pop would only move down here and bring Jimmy, all would be jake.

About coming home: I have turned my name into the shipping office. When a boat shows up, I'll only know a day ahead. But if you insist, I can come home—take a chance on another boat.

[t] Billy

Thursday

[1]McClure's generally positive review of *The Marble Faun* appeared in his Sunday column "Literature—and Less" on January 25, 1925.

[2]The New Orleans friend on the staff of the *Double Dealer* to whom Faulkner dedicated the sonnet: "The Faun/To H.L."

To Mrs. M. C. Falkner   [postmarked 27 Jan. 1925]
[env]   [New Orleans]

Here's John McClure's review. Please let Phil see it. I et so
heavy last night at Mrs. Marcus'[1] that I aint I'm feeling a
mite off today. I hope to recover enough to wield a fork
tonight, though. I am alsono sending a letter I received the
other day. Too bad grandfather wasn't a movie actress—she
could have described her appearance, too.

All right, I'll come home about the middle of Feb., for a
while. Golfed again yesterday. It was just like spring.

Billy

[1]Lillian Friend Marcus was managing editor and one of the founders, with her
brother Julius Weis Friend, of the *Double Dealer*.

To Mrs. M. C. Falkner   [late Jan. 1925]
                                                      [New Orleans]

Dear Mother—
    I have turned in 5 of my sketches stories and collected
$20.00 for them. I write one in about 3 hours. At that rate I
can make $25.00 a week in my spare time. Grand, isn't it?
They want some short things—about 200 words with a kick
at the end. I can knock off one of them while I'm waiting for
my teakettle to boil. They pay $1.00 for each of them. The
others run so much a column. I believe, if I'd work eight
hours a day at it, I could earn $50.00 a week. That is, as long
as they take them. The first will appear in the Sunday magazine a week from next Sunday. I am trying to get a contract
at, say $10.00 per week, while I am touring Europe, with
him. I have told you Col. Edmonds is going to give me a

contract when I get back, haven't? He thinks the trip abroad will be the making of me, that I can write something no other paper can duplicate exactly. $20.00. Hot dog. When I get established with him, I'm going to dump all that stuff I have scribbled and left at home, on him. All's well, and the twilight is like spring—vague azure and green and silver.

Billy

OVER.

I have had two more letters from strange females who saw my photo in the paper.[1] One about 40, gushing, you know; and the other about 14—on pink paper and terrible spelling.

Pepys cost $6.00.[2] No, I have got no check from you for it. I gave my own money for it.

---

[1] The publicity photo of Faulkner that Stone made for *The Marble Faun* appeared in the *Times-Picayune* early in 1925 over the legend "Southern Poet in New Orleans."

[2] This is the first of two editions of Pepys Faulkner purchased for his mother in the spring of 1925. The second he sent from Memphis in late February following his trip home to Oxford.

To Mrs. M. C. Falkner   [early Feb. 1925]
[New Orleans]

Dear Mother—

I got the check. And I have committed something unique in the annals of American literature—I sold a thing to The Double Dealer for cash money, money you can buy things with, you know.[1] There is only one other person in history to whom The Double Dealer has paid real actual money to, and that man is Sherwood Anderson. Fame, stan' by me. Its him and me f'um now on. When Elizabeth saw the check, she threw up her hands and shrieked. It simply aint done, here, to be paid regular money by that magazine. So many folks are wild to break into print, you see, and they dont have to. I had a grand letter from that Arkansas dame yesterday. She sent me her picture, and wants me to suggest a name for her dog. I wrote her to name it Fido.

Billy

[1]Faulkner was paid $10 for the eleven vignettes that compose "New Orleans," which appeared with his poem "Dying Gladiator" and his essay "On Criticism" in the *Double Dealer* for January-February 1925. He is mistaken in claiming to be the only writer except Anderson to be paid by the magazine.

To Mrs. M. C. Falkner   [early Feb. 1925]
                                           [New Orleans]

Dear Mother—
   The candy arrived. What with boxes of fudge from home and the dinners Elizabeth cooks for us, I believe I am getting fat, instead of lean. She certainly is grand to me—she absolutely put her foot down on my paying board at all—lets me stay here and buys marmalade for my breakfast, and cooks dinner every night. She keeps my money for me and only gives me $1.00 at a time so I wont lose or spend it.
   My series of stories in the Times-Picayune begins next Sunday. I will try to subscribe to the Sunday paper for you, so you can get them. They'll be in the Sunday Magazine Section. The funny thing is, I am gaining quite a reputation here. People call to see me, and invite me out, and I sit and look grand and make wise remarks. Another local paper has my picture today. I am sending it along to you.
   By the way, when my series of stories begins, please keep the copies I send you, and we can make a scrap book of them some day.

I see Harry Rainold and Russell Pigford[1] and Norwin Harris, whom I knew in the R.A.F. occasionally. In fact, I see more nice people than I can find time for. I spend the mornings writing and the afternoons walking around, watching the kids around the hand-organs in the parks, or at the Museum looking at the pictures, and the evenings talking with painters and writers and musicians. Did you get the review of the book John McClure wrote for the paper? You havent mentioned getting it yet. *Be sure and keep it.*

I'm getting along so well here that I am still putting off going abroad. I will come home about the middle of this month, and then get ready to go. Boys from here—painters and writers, are always going over, working their way; like folks at home go to Memphis. And most of the freight boats sailing from here have arrangements like hotels, so much a day for the trip. So even the girls can go.

How is every one?

Billy

[1]Russell Pigford was a member of Sigma Alpha Epsilon fraternity with Faulkner at the University of Mississippi, 1919–1920. Pigford was studying medicine in New Orleans.

To Mrs. M. C. Falkner   [7 Feb. 1925]
                                       [New Orleans]

Dear Mother—

Sherwood has sent me a grand tie, R.A.F. regimental colors, from New York.[1] I am all dressed up now. It goes so well with my gray suit: dark blue, gray, scarlet, gray, and dark blue again.

Last night I went to Victor's for dinner. It's one of those old established restaurants that has changed hands several times. The present owner is an Italian, named Guido. I go there—a small place, mostly people he knows personally, who dine and talk, all for 50¢. Soup, fish, meat, salad, fruit and coffee. Last night his "waitress" told me her particular story, she's from Florida, about being married and deserted, and ect, as Ring Lardner says; and when everyone had gone, Guido came in and asked me to have a glass of wine with him. And he told me his story. His father, it seems, was a duke (since the Medici's a wop duke is not anything, you know) and his older brother inherited the title, and dashed little else. So Guido comes to America— "grrrand contree, when I come. But now she ruin herself with prohibition." He'd get excited and lapse into Italian and French at a great rate. "Liberty, hell," he'd say, "man come in, eat—'Che spendo yo, Combien de?' that's all." I suggested to him that money is not such a bad thing, taken by and large. "Monnee?" he says, completely dashing my theory, "Plus d'argent, moins d'argent; coma es'?" quoting a stanza of Dante, stuff about the simple heart, and living on acorns.

I got the check. Thank you.

It is like spring, today. Sky all full of fat white clouds like little girls dressed up and going to a party,
[Holograph postscript]
I will subscribe to the paper for you. The first one appears to-morrow.

Billy.

---

[1]Sherwood Anderson was away from New Orleans on a speaking tour when Faulkner arrived in the city in January. He must have sent the tie from New York in early February when the stage adaptation of his *Triumph of the Egg* opened at the Provincetown Playhouse.

To Mrs. M. C. Falkner   [early Feb. 1925]
                                           [New Orleans]

Dear Moms—

I sent you today a Sunday magazine with the first of my series.[1] I will subscribe to the paper for you, but let me know if you want the daily, or the Sunday paer. At once, so I can fix it.

I am like John Rockefeller—when ever I need money I sit down and dash off ten dolars worth for them. I sold them 30.00 worth, and the Double Dealer 10.00 already yet, as Mrs Friedman would say. They know that someday I'll be a "big gun" and they are glad to get it.

I am getting along grand. Plenty of good food—Elizabeth sees to that—and sleep, and so on. In fact, I feel so prosperous that I am thinking of buying a pair of shoes.

De sure and let me know if you need anything here. New Orleans is quite a place, even if it isnt as big as Chicago. The stores keep almost anything you'd need. Show Phil the story, but keep it yourself.

                                           Billy.

[Holograph postscript]

I am writing Mrs Brown a note, thanking her for doing my book at her club. Was Mrs. Brown, or Mrs Bondurant, responsible?[2] Let me know, so I can write the proper one. Arkansas sent me her picture last week. I'm scared of that lady, I dont mind saying.

---

[1]"Mirrors of Chartres Street," *Times-Picayune*, February 8, 1925.

[2]Oxford residents, the wives of University of Mississippi faculty members Calvin S. Brown and Alexander L. Bondurant.

To Mrs. M. C. Falkner   [16 Feb. 1925]
                                           [New Orleans]

Getting on fine. Let me know if you *did not* get yesterday's
paper: I'll send you one.[1]

Right now I am "thinking out" a novel.[2] As soon as I get it
all straight, I will begin work.

I expect to come home this week. I will wire you as soon as I
can just when to expect me.

Let me know if you are getting your paper. We must save
these things.

I had a note from Natalie[3], which I am sending you.

I answered the same day.

                                                    Billy

No, I have lost Natalie's note. She had seen Aunt Bama[4] in
Memphis, and she was congratulating *you and me* on the
book. Said you simply would not write to her. Why dont
you write her, you lazy thing.

[1]Faulkner's second sketch, "Damon and Pythias Unlimited," was published in the
Times-Picayune February 15, 1925.
[2]This is the earliest notice of Faulkner's first novel, *Soldiers' Pay* (1926).
[3]Natalie Carter Broach, elder daughter of Faulkner's great-aunt Willie Medora
Falkner Carter.
[4]Faulkner's great-aunt Alabama Leroy Falkner McLean, youngest sister of Willie
Medora.

To Mrs. M. C. Falkner Friday [20 Feb. 1925]
[env] [New Orleans]

What's the trouble, moms? I know something is wrong from your last letter.

I think I'll leave here Monday. I have held off wrinting so as to be able to tell you definitely. I'll say when as soon as I can know.

Carnival began last night, with floats and masques and colored fire. The street was hung with colored lights and all traffic stopped for three hours. A people! gosh. I got caught on the wrong side and thought I'd never get home.

A plane with a wing-walker has been over here, and a whole grade of little school boys are doing Nature in the park. Just like spring today, simply grand. More later.

[no signature]

To Mrs. M. C. Falkner [probably 28 Feb. 1925]
Hotel Gayoso
Memphis

Dear Mother—

I sent you today a good Pepys—in two volumes, the next best to the 20 volume original. Stark's poems are not to be had.[1] I had hoped to leave here today, but I am trying to collect 100 dollars from a reluctant debtor, and I will go tomorrow afternoon. What a fearful hole Memphis is! I dont see how in the world you like the place.

God bless you and keep you, and dont let those old cats

bother you. I'll write Monday or Tuesday from New Orleans.

With love,
Billy.

You should get the books Monday.

¹Stark Young's book of poems, *The Blind Man at the Window*, was published in 1906.

To Mrs. M. C. Falkner
[env]

[postmarked 3 Mar. 1925]
Leonardi Studios
520 Saint Peter St.
New Orleans

Dear Mother—
Arrived safely. Elizabeth has not returned yet.¹ They expect her today. I will send you an address as soon as I can. Anything important you might send to the old address.— 540 B. St. Peter.

Billy.

¹ Elizabeth Anderson was in Chicago to accompany her husband home after his speaking tour. She was a partner, with Marc Antony, in the interior decorating firm Leonardi Studios.

To Mrs. M. C. Falkner
[env]

[postmarked 5 Mar. 1925]
[New Orleans]

Dear Mother—
The cake came yesterday and we had some of it for supper last night. Sherwood said, after seeing the handkerchiefs

and eating a piece of the cake, that he certainly would like to know my mother.

I am staying with Bill Spratling[1] now, whose address is 624 Orleans Alley. You can address me here until I write you otherwise. I am going down today to get Pop's pen and to see about a boat, but I shall be here a week probably, yet.

Billy

[1]New Orleans painter and instructor in architecture at Tulane University. In July 1925, Spratling accompanied Faulkner to Europe.

To Mrs. M. C. Falkner   [early March 1925]
                                       [New Orleans]

Dear Mother—

Sherwood and I are writing a book together.[1] He, of course, insists that I wait until it is finished before going abroad. And I may wait that long. I dont know, though; the boat I want to take is due in any day now.

I have a nice room. There are two of us—Piper, a newspaper man, and I. We have two rooms, a court and a kitchen on the ground floor of a lovely paved alley facing the garden of St Louis cathedral—the best spot in New Orleans in which to live. The garden has an iron fence, and trees, and children play in it all day. Elizabeth has loaned me a cot and bedding, and I have my tea kettle, so I am in good shape. We will move in tomorrow.

I am writing a novel of my own, helping Sherwood write our mutual book, beside my Chartres street series. They start again next sunday, I think.[2] I also wrote today an article on "What is wrong with marriage?" for the Times.[3] In fact, I have more stuff than I can get time to write.

My love to everyone.

[t] Billy.

[1]Almost certainly some form of the tall-tale "Al Jackson Letters" that Faulkner and Anderson exchanged at this time. The book was never completed, but Faulkner incorporated some of the tales into his novel *Mosquitoes* (1927), set in New Orleans.

[2]The *Times-Picayune* series did not resume with the fifth sketch, "Cheest," until April 5, 1925.

[3]"What Is Wrong with Marriage" was published in the New Orleans *Item-Tribune*, April 4, 1925, and won Faulkner a $10 first prize for the best short essay on that subject.

To Mrs. M. C. Falkner   [postmarked 8 March 1925]
[env]   624 Orleans Alley
     N.O., La

Bill Spratling's house faces the garden behind St Louis Cathedral. The Catholics, you know, have a mass each hour from 6 o'clock to nine, and then a big one at 11 o'clock. Across the garden is the house where the priests live. They are pretty nice men—Bill knows several of them. The nuns live in a wing of the same house—a convent. Between masses the little choir boys in their purple robes and white surplices play leap frog in the garden, yelling and cursing each other, then go back inside and sing like angels.

The weather is still like spring, clear and warm, and young silver leaves in all the trees. golly, I miss the hills and fruit trees and things now. Think of all that grand country to walk and ride through, and yet folks will make their homes in a city! I feel like now I'd like to build me a log cabin out on Woodson ridge, and just set.

The boat is delayed. Bill had a card from the Captain yesterday, mailed at Athens. It will not be in before the 15th. Wish I had known that: I could have stayed at home longer.

Will you please send my golf clubs. Get them off tomorrow, if it is possible. Put the white bag in the big one, and get the key and lock it. If you cant find the key, get Sonny[1] to tie it up good and insure it.

My love to every body.

Billy.

[1]J. W. "Sonny" Bell, Jr., succeeded Faulkner as university postmaster.

To Mrs. M. C. Falkner [postmarked 11 March 1925]
[env] 624 Orleans Alley
N.O., La.

Dear Mother and Dad—

I received the cake, the clothes, the money order and the clubs. I think the cake is all right. And I know Bill Spratling does. We eat it, anyway. I am glad the pen suits. The point is interchangeable, you know, and if that one is not satisfactory, I can get another one put in. It is a good pen, but for 7.50 you deserve to be thoroughly satisfied. So if it is not, send it back, the salesman told me.

Elizabeth sends love. She has just had influenza, but she is up again. And then Sherwood had it. Dad should see some of the shirts and ties he has. Loud is no word. He says he likes colors and he dont give a hoot who knows it. He has a green corduroy shirt, and more red and orange and yellow ties! He looks like an electric sign when he is dressed up.

It is like summer here, almost. People going around in shirt sleeves, and the trees all with leaves on them. By the way, Anita Loos (Mrs. J. Emerson) the one who does scenarios for the movies, is here, to visit Sherwood.[1] She is rather nice, quite small—I doubt if she is five feet tall. Looks like a flapper. But she and Emerson get $50,000.00 for photoplays. I'd look like Harry Lundie for $50,000.

I will try today to find Mother some blonde shoes. That was all right, giving the marmalade to John.[2] Sending money for it. With much, much love. Gosh, I'm homesick for the hills today.

Billy.

[1]Anita Loos is the author of the satiric Hollywood novel *Gentleman Prefer Blondes* (1925). Her husband, the actor-director John Emerson, was a boyhood friend of Anderson's in Clyde, Ohio.
[2]The third Falkner brother, John Wesley Thompson Falkner III.

To Mrs. M. C. Falkner [postmarked 18 March 1925]
[env] [New Orleans]

Dear mother—

I am looking for shoes for you today. I was about Saturday (I didn't get the old shoe until then) but no luck. I will send you something, though.

Piper (the newspaper man) and I have a whole floor two rooms, a caourt and a kitchen. My room gives directly onto the alley beside the St Louis cathedral garden, and Bill Spratling the painter who lives above us, gives us breakfast and lets us use his bath room. SO his maid servant, a colored Lady yclept Eleanora calls us at breakfast time, and cleans up for us while we eat. This is the best part of town to live in, I think. Quiet and peaceful, and the grass and the trees in the cathedral garden just outside my door. And only about five minutes (walking) from Canal street. Isn't it funny, how

comfortable any place you call your own, is? I can come and
go when I like, sleep as long as I please, invite whom I like to
come to see me—its grand.

Spratling has done another portrait of me. Everyone says
it is the best thing he has ever done. I am going to havw it
photographed and send you a copy. It is good drawing, but
not such a good likeness. The face has more force and character than I have, I think.

I have been taken up by the wealthy jews, lately. They
have good food; and Marjorie Gumble[1] is quite nice. Her
mother is a gentile and her father a jew: they live in Holland
because they like the food. Sherwood cant stand them anymore. He likes Margie, but Elizabeth wont let him have
anything to do with any of them.He is always saying to me
"how cant you stand them?" Of course my reply is "I am
not married."

Moms, Please send me two towels, bath towels.
I will write again about the shoes.

[t] Billy

(Margie Gumble has got a fat little girl, kind of like Jimmy)

---

[1]Margery Kalom Gumble. Her husband, Irving Gumble, was a New Orleans securi-
ties broker who had contributed a review to the *Double Dealer*.

To Mrs. M. C. Falkner   [late March 1925]
                                  [New Orleans]

Dear Mother:—
Saturday Sherwood chartered a gasoline yacht and about
12 of us went across Lake Ponchartrain and up a river. The
lake is big—26 miles, and from the middle of it you cant see
any land. The crew was the captain, the pilot, and an En-

glish steward, and me to plot the course on a chart and navigate. We left at ten, stopped off Mandeville and went swimming, then ate lunch and danced on deck and played cards until tea. The we tied up and walked about till dinner. Danced some more and bed. The men folks slept on deck, on mattresses. It turned cold over night, but was fair the next day as we went up the river. I turned out about six oclock. The shores were all swamp, ducks and geese all around, and owls hooting from the moss-covered cypress trees, and alligators bellowing way back in the lagoons. The water is not muddy, like ours, but black as ink. Anything could be in it. About eight we stopped again. The captain runs the engine, the pilot steers and I handled the anchor and lines. We got a bucket of live bait here, and picked up a river pilot, went on further to an old wharf and tied up to fish. The swamps are full of big yellow wild honeysuckle blooms, and some red things, I dont know what trees they bloom on. We caught a few fish, and I spent most oof the day rowing in a skiff. After lunch another fellow and I took the skiff and pulled back down the river and the boat came along and picked us up.

The wind had been pretty high all day, and the captain told us to look out for a rough lake passage. We went swimming again, and just after tea we got into rough water. the boat heaved and rolled; and it was funny when we went down to dinner, swaying and pitching, to see folks take one look at the food and say "Guess I'll go on deck: I am not hungry." So the rest of us ate, and told each other how we never get sea-sick. I enjoyed the rough going—the hissing sound the waves made all curling and whipped to white spray, and the roll and surge of the boat and the black sky. We got in at nine—best time I've in days.

The captain (Dean) would go wild here, with all these ducks. Mallards, teal, and a black duck that gets so fat he cant leave the water, just flaps along heavily in circles, dragging his feet. Of course, he isn't good to eat.

Those alligators sould like dragging a heavy plank across the top of an empty barrel.

Sherwood and I have invented a grand character—Al Jackson, grandson of Old Hickory. We spent the whole tim trip making up stories about him. We are going to make a book of him. You know, kind of like Sut Lovingood.[1] Here's a few of them. He was on a boat at the mouth of pearl river once, at night, and a shoal of fish came in so thick that he could hear tgeir scales scraping together. He though the boat was sinking and jumped overboard, but the surface of the water was so rigid with fish that he broke his leg.

Once he was in the courtry with nothing but a horse. He needed a night's sleep badly so he found a man who would swap him a night's sleep for the horse. But the man never did show up—left him there all night holding the horse.[2]

He got his start in life as a fish-herd for the game commission. He worked once in the California frog ranches and is web-footed. So he can outswim the fish—run the old maverick fish down, see, and drive them back into the herd. He marks them by putting a notch in the tails. Whenever you see a fish with a notched tail, Al Jackson once owned him.

We are going to sell it and buy a boat with the proceeds.

[t] Billy

---

[1]Tall-tale hero of George Washington Harris's *Sut Lovingood, Yarns* (1867).

[2]In his 1925 review "Sherwood Anderson" in the Dallas *Morning News*, and in his 1953 essay "A Note on Sherwood Anderson," Faulkner attributed this experience to Anderson himself. The Anderson correspondence indicates that Anderson was the originator of the tale.

To Mrs. M. C. Falkner   [postmarked 26 March 1925]
[env]   [New Orleans]

Dear mother—

I sent your shoes to you. You have the priviledge of returning them. I am also sending you areproduction of the
sketch Bill did of me.

Getting along grand. Anita Loos hires a big car and takes
us riding almost everyday. We went out to Chalmette yesterday, where the battle of New Orleans was fought, saw the
old house where the British General, Packenham,[1] lived,
and an avenue of moss-hung oaks three hundred years old,
with the river at the end of them.

I had a book review on the book page of last Sunday's
Times-Picayune. Of Ducdame, by Powys.[2]

Love to all.

[t] Billy

[1]American forces under Andrew Jackson defeated the British, under Lieutenant
General Sir Edward Pakenham, in a battle fought on the grounds of the Chalmette
plantation on January 8, 1815. Pakenham's headquarters were at Villere Plantation.
[2]Faulkner's review of John Cooper Powys's novel *Ducdame* appeared in the *Times-
Picayune* on Sunday, March 22, 1925.

To Mrs. M. C. Falkner   [postmarked 31 March 1925]
[env]   [New Orleans]

Dear Mother—

I got the cake and bacon and cheese. Us et them. Yes, the
story of Mr Anderson's was started by me.[1] It is not docu-
mentary—that is, a true incident. I just kind of cranked him
up. What really happens, you know, never makes a good
yarn. You have got to get an impulse from somewhere and
then embroider it. And that is what Sherwood did in this

case. He has done another about me as I really am, not as a fictitious character. He is now writing a book about childhood, his own childhood;[2] and I have told him several things about my own which he is putting in as having happened to him.

I am now giving away the secrets of our profession, so be sure not to divulge them. It would be kind of like a Elk or a Mason or a Beaver or something giving away the pass word. This thing he is doing now, the childhood thing, he has a contract for. He expects about—I think he said—seven thousand dollars for. Someday, I'll be that good. In secret, remember. He and I are getting our book along, and I am writing one of my own, a novel.

Can you spare me some sheets? If not convenient, I can buy them here. Two, if you can.

I got the twoels all right.

[t] Billy

[1]"A Meeting South," where Faulkner is depicted as an alcoholic wounded aviator. Faulkner first met Anderson in late 1924. The story appeared in the *Dial*, April 1925.
[2]*Tar: A Midwestern Childhood* (1926) was Anderson's first book for his new publisher, Boni & Liveright.

To Mrs. M. C. Falkner   [early April 1925]
                                 [New Orleans]

Dear Mother:—
    My novel is going splendidly. I put in almost 8 hours a day on it—I work so much that the end of my "typewriting" finger is like a boil all the time. Sherwood read a chapter, says its good stuff, and is helping me try to sell it to Mr Liveright, of Boni & Liveright, who is here now trying to get

Sherwood's next book. Sherwood thinks that if he will take it we can get an advance on it as soon as he accepts it. Which will be elegant, hey Al?

I have just written a story which I am today sending to the di Dial, and another story which the Times-Picayune has taken. I have been to busy to write any Chartres street lately. I have gotten permission from Col. Edmonds to submit the Chartres street things, after he has printed them, to another newspaper, a northern one. Think I'll try the Boston "Transcript." Spratling has also done some sketches and we intend trying to get them out in book form.[1]

Getting along fine. I have met two girls with cars which they let me drive. I got the—wait and let me open it—the sheets. Thank you. By the way, I saw a fine movie "He Who Gets Slapped," with Lon Chaney. Make bob Williams get it.[2] You never did say if the shoes were satisfactory. And has the captain found Lee's tent?

I dreamed last night that I waked and there was Jimmy, sitting on my table with his duck.

[t] Bill

Will you please fill in this application for a birth certificate have it witnessed, and send it to me?

---

[1] A year later, Faulkner and Spratling collaborated on *Sherwood Anderson & Other Famous Creoles*, privately printed, consisting of Spratling's sketches of New Orleans people and a foreword by Faulkner parodying Anderson's style.

[2] Robert X. Williams managed the Oxford movie theater. He was married to Faulkner's cousin Sallie Murry Wilkins.

To Mrs. M. C. Falkner [postmarked 7 April 1925]
[env] [New Orleans]

Moms, dear heart, I just opened the parcel tonight. Sheets soap and tooth paste—enough for anyone. That's all I need. Piper (the newspaper man with whom I am living) has some linen, enough for us. He is quite young—he tells me about his mother, and how old he is, and how he likes New Orleans. He is from Illinois, only child. His father is dead. Funny kind of a boy. He has the strangest admiration for me. Makes me feel like I ought to do something quite grand for his sake. Like saving the child in the burning building, or capturing a burglar, or going into the movies. Or maybe I should be a fireman in a red shirt and a two gallon oil-cloth hat. Anyway, I know I am not doing what he thinks I ought to. But then the law-breaking and heroic market is so crowded these days.

Spratling has done a sketch and I have written a story which we are sending off tomorrow.[1] Sherwood says it is a rotten story. But then he may be right. I think it is pretty good, myself. Maybe he doesn't like it bevause (not for publication) I left the worm out.

Its too bad dad must give up an old and comfortable habit, but I am glad the doctor is making him stay away from that office. There is too much in the world to see, to spend all the time between four walls. Wait until you can get down in this country. You aint seen nothing yet, as the poet says.

[t] Billy

---

[1]Possibly the Spratling drawing of Faulkner that appeared with Faulkner's "Out of Nazareth" on Easter Sunday, April 12 1925. Spratling is named there as one "whose hand has been shaped to a brush as mine has (alas!) not."

To Mrs. M. C. Falkner   [postmarked 10 April 1925]
[env]   [New Orleans]

Dear Moms:

I got the cake. I got the pillow case. I got the review.[1] Cheer up, things aint so bad: I received this morning a letter of appreciation from mr r e little of Blue Mountain, miss. ". . . thought I would write you a letter of appreciation . . . I am glad to see Miss. coming to the front with her native poets . . . gleaned from the review[2] that you have some true poetic lines . . . get your book as soon as possible . . . have read nothing of yours save the exerpts in the review, but I class you far above Wm A Percy.[3] I have read several things of his but noticed little song in it."

Its priceless, a gem. We must put it away as soon as Elixabeth and Sherwood see it, I'll send it on to you.

That lady she taken that book and run it through her typewriter any old dam way, didn't she. That's the kind of review I want—to find what is wrong with the stuff. Just to pick out the good "true poetic lines" and ignore the others doesn't do me any good. I can do that myself.

I am writing mr little a letter, sending you a carbon.[4] Let Phil see it.

[t] Billy

---

[1]Miss Monte Cooper's negative review of *The Marble Faun* appeared in the Memphis *Commercial-Appeal*, April 5, 1925.

[2]Mr. Little's letter was in response to John McClure's *Times-Picayune* review of *The Marble Faun*, January 25, 1925.

[3]William Alexander Percy, Greenville, Mississippi, poet and essayist. Faulkner's own mixed review of Percy's poems, *In April Once*, appeared in *The Mississippian*, November 20, 1920.

[4]Enclosure: To Mr E. Little, esq.; TcarbonLS, n.d.:
Dear Mr Little:—
Your kind note was today forwarded to me here. I am glad to know that ~~my~~ the labor of Mississippi poets is appreciated in Blue Mountain. Having one's work appreciated by the people of one's native state makes the labor well worth while. If your

sentiments regarding the poets of Mississippi were only more general through the state, there is no reason why Mississippi should not produce verse as good as that of any state in the Union.

Thank you for your (to me) very kind comparison ~~with~~ of my work with that of Mr Percy.

Sincerely,

[s] William Faulkner

Wm Faulkner
624 Orleans alley
New Orleans, la.

To Mrs. M. C. Falkner [postmarked 13 April 1925]
[env] [New Orleans]

Dear Mother—

Last week was holy week. Lent was over at noon Saturday. Thursday was Holy Thursday, Friday the fun began. They held masses all day long in the cathedrals, all the stores were closed. The "rookery" across the way was like a nest of crowns all day, with black-robed priests flitting in and out, and the Archbishop in his scarlet nightie with people stopping to kisshis ring. And the choir boys in scarlet robes and lace surplices fighting and playing leap-frog and cursing between masses, then going in to sing like angels, and returning to finish the fight.

I went to the evening mass. The candles were all lighted, and incense, and saints and the Virgin all about. People in Catholic churches sit in their pews and whenever they want to pray, they kneel whether anyone else wants to or not. When they enter they dip their fingers in the holy water basin and cross themselves, then when they pass the altar they bow.

Ther service is all in latin, chanted by the priests—the St Louis cathedral is a big one: they have about thirty priests.

Nobody ever preaches: its all music. Grand to watch, and how those little boys can sing!

People go and come as they like. The churches are open all day long and someone is always going in to kneel before the Virgin a few moments. And all Catholics go—you never see a Catholic who doesn't go to church at least once a day.

I have written three short stories, and am half way through my novel. Going some, what. There is a lady of about 30 who has taken a shine to me. I have to waste some time evading her. ~~But then man's life was never a bed of roses.~~ One of those intense ones: empress of stormy emotions. But then man's life is never a bed of roses. If it aint mosquitoes its something else.

[t] Billy

To Mrs. M. C. Falkner   [postmarked 16 April 1925]
[env]   [New Orleans]

Dear Mother:—

Will you please send that old gray coat which I left hanging in my closet? It is getting too hot here for my heavy clothes.

I am in a writing slump now—cant seem to do anything. Have it all in my head but cant put it on paper for some raeson. Stale, I guess.

I am glad to hear about the captain's team.

Sonny will change his mind now, about how easy it is to run a post office. It is no bed ofroses by a damsight. He thought all the time that I just sat there and loafed between trains. Hope he pulls through all right. I'd kind of like to hear Prof Bell[1] on the subject.

I am about half through with my novel. Elizabeth and Sherwood both say it is a good one.

[t] billy

'University of Mississippi Professor James Warsaw Bell, whose son Sonny Bell succeeded Faulkner as university postmaster.

To Mrs. M. C. Falkner   [postmarked 20 April 1925]
[env]   [New Orleans]

Dear Moms:—

I have so much to tell you I dont know where to start. It is about a Scotsman. You know, it takes a Britisher to really "go bad" The American can always be reformed by talk of home and mother, but when a Britisher is bad, he's bad. This man's name is Collins.[1] His people are publishers in ~~Edi~~ Glasgow. I haven't heard his whole story yet, but I think he must have done something that made him leave England. He is a big man, with a long Scottish chin and reddish sandy hair, about thirty five or maybe forty.

Anyway, he was not in England when the war broke out, but came home and (he had in some way gotten a Colonel's commission in the British marines) transferred to a Scottish outfit. The took him because of his clan, I imagine, and he commanded a battalion at Gallipoli, one of the bloodiest battles of the war, against the Turk in 1914. He wont talk about it, but someone who knows him says that he has several decorations and that his men were crazy about him— followed him around like dogs.

He was wounded and was sent to Canada in 1918 as C.O. at Valcartier, an army post. After the war he ran off with somebody's wife (he had been married once and divorced) to India and there he got mixed up in a jewel scandal of some sort. He, of course, says he bought it, and some say he stole it. Anyway, he ran to New Orleans with his lady friend, and the government got him. He spent a year in a Louisiana jail, his lady friend, whom he had married, divorced him, and he was down on his luck.

Then he took up the horse racing game, got in with some gamblers and made a hundred thousand dollars, bought a yacht and splashed around considerable. He got married again, to a New York girl, who left him right off and is now getting a divorce from him. But no one seems to know exactly what he has done. Anyway he cant go home. He is rather a nice sort, good manners, educated, but just "bad" He is very nice to have around, though. Doesn't talk about himself at all: quite pleasant. He has taken a shine to me, lately, comes for me in his car, a Cadillac, and we golf and swim together. He seems to be quite impressed that I am a writer.

Yesterday afternoon, Mrs Marcus, the Double Dealer lady, a girl named Flo Something² and Mrs Gumble (she is the nicest one I have met. She is twenty four and has the most beautiful hair I ever saw. It is really gold—sometimes it looks yellow and sometimes it is red, like a gold coin. There is something about the shape of her forehead and eyes that reminds me of you) went s and Colonel Collins and another bird and I went swimming. then we went to Mrs Gumble's for dinner, and about eleven Collins and I went to the Artists' Ball, a masquerade dance. More funny folks, all breaking their necks trying to have a good time. After the dance Collins and I went to a cabaret where they have a nigger band, to get something to eat, then home.

This afternoon he came around to see me. I biled up some tea for him and he smoked his pipe and chatted a while. I want to get the straight of that jewel business. It will make a corking story, I bet. I wrote a funny story yesterday. I have been chuckling about it ever since. When I get it copied off I will send you one.

I hope to gtt to work onmy novel again tomorrow. I have been stale all this week.

When you get around to it, will you send my "ice-cream" striped pants, and that gray Norfolk coat I borrowed from dean. It is hot here. ~~And my linen suit. No hurry just when it is convenient.~~

[Holograph] And my linen knickers.

[no signature]

¹Charles Glenn Collins was the model for Colonel Ayers in Faulkner's *Mosquitoes* (1927).

²Flo Field wrote one-act plays and organized the first guide service in the French Quarter.

To Mrs. M. C. Falkner   [postmarked 23 April 1925]
[env]   [New Orleans]

Dear Moms:—

I got the clothes allright—and just in time. Old thermometer runs up to 90 here without half trying.

I have got a dog-gone good novel. Elizabeth and Sherwood both say so. Sherwood says he wishes he had thought of it first. They have taken me in charge, wont even let me read anything until I finish it. It has the war for a background. Two men who didn't get overseas, and for whom the war stopped too soon, and one man who was missing in action, his father gave him up, and then he turns up at home so badly hurt taht he dies. The war didn't stop soon enough for him, you see. His father has to go through the whole thing twice. Mother is dead. There are two women, one who helped him get home—he is going blind and his mind is deranged, and the one he was engaged to who sees his scarred face and throws him down.

I hope to have it finished by the end of June. And Sherwood is going to try to make his publisher take it and give me an advance on it, the book to appear next fall.

Getting along fine. My money will carry me safely through June, and then I will get a job until the publisher comes across. When you get time, send my linen suit—the two pants one. I will send my tweeds home.

[t] Billy

To Mrs. M. C. Falkner　　　[postmarked 1 May 1925]
[env]　　　　　　　　　　　[New Orleans]

Dear Moms—

I got the cake today, a grand one. I think it is the best one yet. Just as fresh and firm, and the icing good and bitter and rich. Couldn't have done better myself.

Frederick O'Brien, the South Sea traveller, is here visiting Mr Anderson. He is a funnly like gray headed Irishman, lively as a cricket. Awful talker: tells one story after another. You know that are mostly lies, but they are interesting. He wrote a book "Whit Shadows of the South Seas"[1] and had done scenario for the movies. Lives in California now. He and Sherwood and I sit and talk until all hours.

There was a terrible man came the other day looking for me. He was from the Palmer Institute in Hollywood Cal. They teach you to write. He had got my name somewhere and he insisted on coming in. I was busy so I said I wasn't the one. "Oh, yes. we have a letter from you in our office. You are the one."

He insisted, bland and blithe as you please, and so I got

mad after a while and decided to fix him. He sat down and said "Now, Mr Faulkner, you want to write, so I'll tell you how to go about it."

I said all right, but to excuse me a moment. I ran up to Spratling's room and dug up a bottle of licker. He refused. No, no he couldn't think of it. I said I am a fiery hot blooded southerner and a stranger could not come in my home and refuse a drink. He became kibd of nervous, lots of laughing, etc. and he poured out just about what he could have put in his eye. Then he asked for water so I went out the door and came back right quick, just as he was going to throw it out. I told him if he threw it out I'd break his damn neck. I filled his glass up good, he protesting, and made him drink it. Then he said You have one and I told him Inever touched it and filled his glass again. He was trying to get out, so I'd hold the door knob, still talking to him. He had to drink again and then he told me about the madam "best little woman in the world" and his 16year old daughter waiting for him downtown. Then after I pressed another drink on him he told me what a fine little woman she was again and how pretty his daughter was and how he just couldn't bring a yung girl down here where artists live—"You know what artists are, no offense, of course?—and how he liked me and was coming back tomorrow. I promised to take him to see a struggling writer named Anderson who would be crazy to take his course, and then ran him out. He didn't come back, either, after swearing to me he would. I dont know what the best little woman in the world did to him. I hope it was a plenty, though.

Jimmy must be kind of funny and fat, walking and talking. I will finish my book this month, and I may come home for a time, unless I fall into something too good to pass up. I expect to be fed up with writing for a while then. Think I'll like to do some out-door work, like farm labor.

My shoulders are all right, moms.² You see, when I have
worked all morning my back is so cramped that I get out
and rear back almost as much as grandfather, and walk six
or eight miles. I expect I am straighter than I was at home.
And I fear I am getting fat.

[t] Billy

¹Frederick O'Brien's *White Shadows in the South Seas* was published in 1919.
²Maud Falkner was so concerned about her son's posture that when he was thirteen
and fourteen she made him wear a whalebone corset to keep him erect.

To Mrs. M. C. Falkner   [early May 1925]
                                 [New Orleans]

Dear Moms
    I got the cake and candy, linen suit, linen pants and
lounging robe. When I saw the robe I thought you had gone
and bought it, but when I examined the seams and those
cuffs and collar I knew youcouldn't buy one like that. So i
put it on to the admoration of all and sundry.
    I sent by express a suit case containing two coats four
pants, six sox, one knickers, two shirts. Will you send back
the bag? That's what I live in. I had the ex. Co. send for the
bag, so I am sending money for charges. It is C.O.D.
    Getting alongf fine. I have 50000 words on my novel. two
thirds through it. I 80000 words is the goal. Wrote 7000
words in one day this week.
    Mr Jack stone¹ was here yesterday. He invited me to
spend a while with them at Pascagoula this summer.
    Sho is grand eating cake. Give Elizabeth A a hunk of it. It
has turned cold here—and me with all my clothes in Miss.
Glad I kept my trench coat. No, Col Collins is a fact. We
played golf yesterday and he has just this minute called me

and invited me to a party at a Mississippi lady's this afternoon.

God bless you moms, for that robe. If you are taking any snap shots of Jimmy, send me one.

[t] billy

¹William E. "Jack" Stone, Phil Stone's older brother, had a summer home on the Gulf Coast at Pascagoula, Mississippi.

To Mrs. M. C. Falkner   [postmarked 7 May 1925]
[env]   [New Orleans]

Dear Moms—

I got the dollar. Grand news about Jack.¹

Still working on my novel. It is very good. I am about two thirds thruogh—about 50,000 words. I kind of hate to finish it. I know I'll never have so much fun with another one. I dream about the people in it. Like folks I know. Awful quiet here now. I spend the mornings working and the afternoons walking (to keep myself down. I am getting fat, I think) and the evenings in visitng people.

The bag came all right. I gave a tea-party with the cake and cheese and ect. &

God bless you, moms. Love to Pop and my kindest personal regards to the captain.

[t] Billy

¹Faulkner's brother Murry C. Falkner, Jr., joined the FBI in 1925.

To Mrs. M. C. Falkner   [postmarked 12 May 1925]
[env]   [New Orleans]

Dear Moms—

I finished my novel last night. I think I wrote almost
10000 words yesterday between 10:00 am and midnight—a
record, if I did. 3000 is a fair days work. I am kind of sorry.
I never have enjoyed anything as much. I know Ill never
have as much fun with the next one—which by the way I am
all ready to go to work on[1]—when I have had a short holiday. All necessary now is to correct it then have it neatly
typed and send it to the publisher. Piper a newspaper man
and a friend of his are going to help me type it. I am drafting
evebr man woman and child who can use a typewriter into
service.

This is really a record. I started the thing about the time I
sent Phil that Al Jackson wire,[2] and am through the something of May. 80,000 words.

I fell lost this morning. I riz and washed and et and then
by force of habit I ran to my typewriter—and there was
nothing to do. So I think I shall take an oyster lugger that
makes a three day trip down into the Cajan country for
oysters. Little tub of a boat, but it will be a complete change.

Tell the captain I guess I never got that letter he written
me because I cant tell him why, like he ast me two.

Much love
[t] billy

---

[1] Possibly *Elmer*, the unfinished novel on which Faulkner worked in Paris in the
autumn of 1925, or *Mosquitoes*, which he began in Paris and published in 1927.

[2] Faulkner and Anderson could not have invented their tall- tale character Al Jackson until Anderson returned to New Orleans from his speaking tour in early March
1925; Al Jackson is first mentioned in Faulkner's letters in late March. First mention
of the novel is in a letter in mid-February.

To Mrs. M. C. Falkner   [mid-May 1925]
                                 [New Orleans]

Dear Moms—

I have got an entire new "set" of sun-burn—an elegant saddle color, like a swell colored gentleman. I had a fine boat trip and ate well. Mosquitoes are big as sparrows and vicious as tigers though. I smell so rank of mosquito oil it is only by an effort that I can even sleep with myself.

I have started correcting and re-typeing my book. Should be done in two weeks, ready to write another one.

It is fine and cool today, after being so hot. Reminds me of fall, starts me aching for Miss. again.

The cake came in good shape. Thank you.

Tell the captain to keep me posted about the S.S. League. I intend to see some of the games.

Love to everyone.

[t] billy

To Mrs. M. C. Falkner   [postmarked 1 June 1925]
[cnv]   [New Orleans]

Dear Moms—

I have been working all week getting my novel corrected and parts rewritten. I am fairly well satisfied with it now. I expect to get it off this week, soon as Elizabeth and Sherwood read it. I have been so busy I have hardly taken time to eat, even. Just to run around the corner for a loaf of bread and a bottle of milk. And I am still getting fat. I dont know just what my plans are yet, depends on how the book looks after I "lay off" of it for a few days. Mr Jack Stone has invited me to stay a while with him in Pascagoula this month. I shall probably go there and come back home with

Phil after he comes down. I will let you know soon as I can.
Love to everybody.

Billy

About the suit. I have plenty of clothes. A man gave me a
linen suit that was too small for him. Thank you though.

To Mrs. M. C. Falkner   [postmarked 11 June 1925]
[env]   [New Orleans]

We got to Pascagoula Saturday. Sunday I swam and spent
the afternoon in a sail-boat. Its fine, more fun than a car
even. I have learned to sail the boat myself. The boy that
owns it left Monday to go on a camp, so he loaned his boat to
George Lewis, Mrs Stone's brother, and me. At night we get
a gasoline torch and spears and go floundering. A flounder is
the port side of a fish. He has only one side, the left one, and
both of his eyes are on the same side. He lies flat on the
bottom and you walk along in about a foot of water and
spear him. You can see the bottom quite plainly by the
torch light, see crabs and mullet and needlefish, and an
occasional stingeree. A stingeree looks like this— [FIG-
URE][1] and in the middle of his tail he has a stinger that will
lay you up in hospital. He lies on the bottom too and varies
from the size of a hat to that of a barrel top. You spear him
like you do a flounder.

S I came to New Orleans today. Am going back to Pascagoula tomorrow. Sherwood Anderson is all blowed up
over the novel. He has written Liveright two letters about it
and Liveright has written asking me to send it on to him.
Sherwood thinks it is going to be a sensation. I hope so.

The coast is certainly grand now. I wish you and pop and the captain would come down. I have about persuaded Sherwood and Elizabeth to spend the week-end at Pascagoula.

[no signature]

¹Line drawing of a flat, round fish with a long "stinger" tail.

To Mrs. M. C. Falkner   [postmarked 22 June 1925]
[env]   [Pascagoula]

Dear Moms—

I think I have a grand chance to get a boat for Spain on the twentyfourth. I wired Phil to send me some clothes— what I want is my Brown Two pants tweed suit, my knickers and my heavy gray socks and my sweater.

I have been so awful busy getting my novel retyped that I have not even written you ~~atletter~~ a letter. My new Orleans gang of course did not do as much as I had hoped, for I now have their ~~mistakes~~ ~~as~~ well ~~as~~ my own to correct. I am going to finish it by Tuesday and send it off, or bust.

I am in a dreadful stew, of course, between the book and the boat, so please send my clothes which I have listed above *as soon as you hear from Phil.* Wait until he calls for them, though. Then send them to me at my *New Orleans* address. I will write again, a long letter as soon as I get the book off.

Billy

To Mrs. M. C. Falkner   [postmarked 25 June 1925]
[env]   [Pascagoula]

Dear Moms:

I just got your letter dated the tenth. I evidently arent so prominent in Pascagoula as a modest man could wish, am I? Still sailing and swimming: I have a grand mahogany color except where my bathing suit fits. I'm sorry I slipped up about writing, But when you spend most of your time writing words, as long as you are all right you want to take it out in thinking about home—writing letters is like the postman taking a long walk on his day off, or the street car motorman taking a car ride.

As soon as I get my plans straightened out I'll let you know.

Billy

To Mrs. M. C. Falkner   [early July 1925]
                                       [New Orleans]

Dear Moms—

The boat is delayed again, at Galveston or somewhere. It will not be in until the end of the week. Wish I had known this yesterday morning.[1] We are trying now to get on a French boat which is in port here.

I forgot my hair brushes. Will you please send them right away? They are in the bathroom, I think.

I got the wire. God bless you for it. Love to all

Billy

---

[1]Faulkner returned to New Orleans from Pascagoula at the end of June by way of Oxford. The "end of the week" would have been Saturday, July 4; Faulkner and Spratling sailed aboard the *West Ivis* Tuesday, July 7, 1925.

To Mrs. M. C. Falkner   Monday 11:00 P.M.
[env]   [6 July 1925]
                                [New Orleans]

Dear moms—

We are off at last. The boat sails tomorrow, ~~Ty~~ Tuesday
2:00 P.M. And I claim I am the best packer in the world: I
have all my junk in a suit-case and a kit bag, including 500
sheets of paper on which to write to you. I shall keep a diary
going over, put down something each day, if only brite and
fair. At least it will be brite and fair in the diary. And that's
probably about the only place it will be, too. But this is not
the storm month: we expect to have a good crossing. Tell
the captain I'll send him and Pop and Jimmy each a brick of
ice cream from Naples. You dont get any. You aint big
enough yet. I'll send you maybe a pitcher book or a monkey
on a stick. Bill and I have been given by kind friends a
hundred addresses of nice people in Europe who will feed
us—one man here, a Russian prince who is related to three
reigning families has given us more highnesses and excellen-
cies than we can see in a year.[1] So all we got to do is set on
the cowcatcher of the steamboat and let the proud world
drift by till she touches the bank, eating heavy and sleeping
light, counting our money while the sailors gnash their teeth
in rage. Quite a gang are coming down to see us off. Hope
they'll have sence enough to bring a band with 'em. I always
have wanted to go some where to the sound of poorly played
cornets and drums. Too bad Jiggetts dont live in N.O.[2] He's
our man.

Remember, we will land on the 30th of July, or there
about.[3] You should hear from me about the tenth of August, or perhaps the fifteenth, allowing for delay, etc. Whatever you do, dont worry unnecessarily. This is one of their
best boats, been making this same voyage every two months

for two years, and a friend of Bill's is to meet us at the dock. So I am much safer than I am every time I cross Canal st. unless Europe rises up on its hind legs and practically falls down on me. Then I'd be so mad I wouldn't care, anyway.

I have picked up about 30.00 dollars for some things since arriving,[4] so I am all right. I wont hesitate to sing out if I need any cash, in plenty of time. So if Europe just stands by me, I'll do her up brown and come home.

Igot my hair brushes alright. Thank you.

Love,
[t] Billy

Monday 11:00 P.M.

---

[1]Among others, a New Orleans banker, grandson of the Russian minister Count Witte, provided an introduction to the Countess Filippo Caracciolo, nee Margaret Clark of New Orleans. In August Faulkner would write that he and Spratling had visited her at Montreux.

[2]Louis M. Jiggetts, a University of Mississippi undergraduate with Faulkner in 1919–1920. Jiggetts was co-author with W.H. Drane Lester of the "Hayseed Letters" which satirized Faulkner as Count No 'Count in *The Mississippian* then. He was a cornetist.

[3]Faulkner debarked at Genoa on August 2; his first letter home is postmarked August 5, 1925.

[4]Possibly some or all of the final four *Times-Picayune* sketches, which appeared after Faulkner's departure: "The Liar" (July 26), "Episode" (August 16), "Country Mice" (September 20), and "Yo Ho and Two Bottles of Rum" (September 27, 1925).

OCTOBER TO
DECEMBER

1925

*F*AULKNER and Spratling arrived in Genoa on August 2, 1925, and traveled together through Italy and Switzerland, where they separated temporarily, Faulkner going to France and arriving in Paris on August 12. Letters published in *Selected Letters of William Faulkner* cover the walking tour and his first two months in Paris, where he lived briefly in a hotel in Montparnasse, then moved to rooms near the Luxembourg Gardens at 26 Rue Servandoni. In late September, after Spratling returned to New York, Faulkner went on a tour of the war zone and early in October crossed the Channel to England, where he spent a week, departing and returning through Dieppe. The letters in the Harry Ransom Center Collection begin with his return to Paris from England and document his last two months in Europe, from October 17 to December 9, and his arrival in New York just before Christmas 1925.

Faulkner had been writing steadily since coming to Paris. By the middle of November he had finished six short stories, half of a novel called *Elmer*, and the opening chapter of *Mosquitoes*. In late September, Spratling had written from New York that Boni & Liveright would publish *Soldiers' Pay*, and Faulkner planned to leave Europe as soon as he received the contract with the advance. However, when it arrived on October 26, he could find no one to cash Liveright's $200 check. The check was returned to America for approval that did not come until early December.

Frustrated by the delay, and angry at Liveright, Faulkner nonetheless could see the humor in his straitened situation. On his return from England, he had dramatized for his mother his difficulties with the French constabulary in Dieppe; now, though he was bitter about Liveright, he wrote in the same vein about the ineptitude of the American Express manager, a Paris policeman, and the American consul. Angry though he was, he seems to have realized that his whole experience in Europe would have deep and long-lasting value for him and for his steadily maturing art. It was in this spirit that he arrived in New York on December 19 ready to go to work on the galleys of his book before turning toward Oxford and home.

To Mr. M. C. Falkner   17 Oct. 1925
[env]   Paris

Dear Dad:—

I returned to Paris today and found your letter. I have just been thinking myself that I have been away from our blue hills and sage fields and things long enough. So I am making arrangements to come home. I will wait here a short time because I am expecting to hear from the publisher, Mr Liveright. But I'll be on the way soon. I have plenty of notes and data to last me a long time: all I need now is to settle down at home comfortable again and bang my typewriter.

I've seen strange people and different things, I've walked a lot in some fine country in France and England, but after all its not like mounting that northeast hill and seeing Woodson's ridge, or the pine hills on the Pontotoc road, or slogging along through those bare fields back of the campus

in a drizzling rain. I am reasonably certain that I'll be on my
way home by Nov. 1.

Much love,
Billy

Paris
17 Oct 1925

To Mrs. M. C. Falkner   21 Oct. 1925
[env]   Paris

Dear Moms—

Getting back to Paris was very nice: next to getting back
to Mississippi will be. I have just had a magnificent dinner,
32¢, at the 3 Musketeers—one of my regular places. The
grilled leg of rabbit (I kidded the waitress about it, but I
dont think it was cat) cauliflower with cheese, figs and nuts
and a glass of wine. The restaurant is kind of a club—a small
place where you see the same people every night: a quiet
young French couple, a lady who wears a colored handker-
chief around her neck and a man's cap, like a bandit, an old
Englishman who has lived in Paris for 50 years, a young
American photographer[1] and myself.

I got arrested again in Dieppe. The 6th time since I've
been in France. I dont know what in the world can look
suspicious about me. It must be that I have a bad face, or
my trench-coat, or something. I certainly wasn't doing anything except standing on the wharf watching a fishing smack
being unloaded, and eating a piece of bread. But here comes
the gendarme on his bicycle.

"Vous papier, monsieur."

"Bien, monsieur." I produce my passport. He opens it upside down.

"Votre etes Anglais?"

"Non, monsieur. Americain." I turn the passport right side up for him.

"Ah-h-h!" he says in a caught-you-at-last tone. He examines the English words on my passport. Then he looks at me again. "Que faites vous, monsieur?"

"Le meme chose que faisent tous des messieurs par la," I respond indicating at least a dozen people who are doing even less than I am.

"Ah-h-h! Alors, venez avec moi au bureau."

It is quite triumphal. He pushes his bicycle, I beside him eating my bread (I have been arrested so often I am blase) While all Dieppe stops doing nothing to come to doors and windows to see, and 3 dirty little boys fall in behind. By the time we reach the "bureau" we have about ten followers. They think I am Lenine, probably; and the sergeant takes my passport from my captor and looks at the English words a long time. They whisper together while the spectators hold their breath. The sergeant says: "You are English?" 'No," I say. "I am American, like the passport says."

"Ah-h-h. What do you make in Dieppe?"

"Nothing. I visit Dieppe meanwhile the march to Paris."

"You go to Paris?"

"But certainly."

"From what place do you come?"

"From London."

"Ah-h-h. And why do you come from London?"

"Because of to go to Paris."

"Ah-h-h." They look at the passport again. Then they look at me again: they've got me now. "On what day do you arrive at Dieppe?"

I give the date and he says, "But it is Switzerland from which you arrive."²

"But one might arrive from Switzerland and also from England in a lifetime. Not so?"

They examine the passport again and the sergeant says: "He departs from Dieppe on the 4 October."

"But he returns," the other pointed out. The sergeant ~~looked~~ stares at me again, at last admitting that I am returned. I am beginning now to ~~agreed~~ with him that only the veriest innocent would ever return to Dieppe. Then the sergeant ~~ma~~ says "Make the examination corporal," and my captor searches me, for bombs, I guess, taking my money, pocket-knife—he takes all. The audience I know are disappointed, but still hopeful they wait while the sergeant takes my possessions into another room with him. He returns without them, and he and my captor sit staring at me for at least 30 minutes. The spectators get tired and drift out, and after a while another cop comes in, with a lot of gold braid on him. He has my passport and he says: "You are writair, monsieur?" "Yes, monsieur." He looks at the passport again. "What is writair, monsieur?" he says, quite kindly. I explain and he says "Ah-h-h! Poet!" he says something quite fast to the others, and I get my things back right now. "You are free, monsieur," he says. "Depart, and bon voyage."

It takes a lot of stupidity to do anything really well, but I t̶h̶l̶ think it requires more down right dullness to be a cop than anything I know.

Still writing. I have a fine collection to bring home with me.

Billy

Paris 21 Oct 1925

[1]The photographer was William C. Odiorne, a friend of Spratling's who had lived in New Orleans before Faulkner arrived there in January 1925. The Englishman may have been a photographer and newspaperman named Sibleigh to whom Odiorne introduced Faulkner that fall.
[2]Faulkner and Spratling arrived in France from Switzerland in mid-August.

To Mrs. M. C. Falkner   26 Oct. 1925
[env]   Paris

No, I'll have to admit I dont have sweet potatoes, nor fresh ham nor hot biscuits either—though I am to soon. The rains have begun—like April. Warm m̶u̶g̶g̶y̶ weather and sunny, then all of a sudden it will rain out of a clear sky almost. You dont dare leave home without a raincoat. This morning though, instead of raining it turned raw and cold, almost too cold to write. The walking days are over until next year, I guess.

I'm writing a story now—the best one yet, as usual. That's the reason writers never get tired and go in the shoe business or something, I imagine. Good for the Captain: I'd much rather he'd be a good football- than a baseball-player. Something to football besides luck and ape-like cleverness—some chance to use your brains (if any) I̶ i̶m̶a̶g̶i̶n̶e̶ h̶e̶'̶s̶ p̶r̶e̶t̶t̶y̶ w̶e̶l̶l̶ p̶o̶l̶i̶s̶h̶e̶d̶ t̶h̶e̶ s̶t̶o̶c̶k̶ o̶f̶ h̶i̶s̶ s̶h̶o̶t̶g̶u̶n̶ How far has he carried his shotgun since the weather turned cool? He's probably fired it over eight times by now, hasn't he? Make him be careful: shooting powder in it will sure wear it out: simply eat the barrel off in 70 or 80 years.

You mustn't let Jimmy get too big until I come home. I want him to be a little boy for a while—until I see him, at least. I've been looking around for something to bring you, and I know exactly what: I will bring you two bird dogs.

Billy

26 Oct 1925

Good news. Just received a contract from Liveright for the novel and an option on the next two I write, and a check for $200.00

To Mrs. M. C. Falkner   30 Oct. 1925
[env]   Paris

Dear Moms—

Liveright sent me a contract. The name of the novel is to be changed,[1] I get $200.00 advance on it and 10% of the first 5000 12 1/2% of the next 5000 and 15% of all above that. He also engages to take the next two novels, giving me $400.00 advance on each, at the same figure, he and I to divide the serial and movie rights. I signed it: of course I'll be his bond slave for two years, but then I guess I'll have to be someone's. So it might as well be him. I have 6 short stories to sell, so my future looks all right financially[2]—only you and Pop will have to furnish the parched corn for a while longer, until the loot starts coming in.

The weather is mild and gray and sunny. Chilly at night, and the leaves are nearly all gone—real Indian summer. Tonight should be the harvest moon. Round and red and warm looking as stale cheese. Riding on 'busses is certainly a vice with me. I spent nearly every afternoon at it—costs me 10¢ a day, too.

I have just finished the 4th best short story in the world— the other 3 being the ones I wrote previous to it.

I think I shall sail for New York the 19th. Must go by and see Liveright. Should be home about Dec. 1st. What ho. Saw a fight, and a small riot, Paris vs Police last night. No casualties, worse luck.

Billy

Paris
30 Oct 1925

¹As Sherwood Anderson's correspondence makes clear, Faulkner's working title for the novel was "May Day." The title change was to *Soldiers' Pay*.

²In fact, Faulkner did not sell his first short story to a national magazine until 1930, when *Forum* bought "A Rose for Emily."

To Mrs. M. C. Falkner   3 Nov. 1925
[env]   Paris

Dear Moms:—

I sail on the 19th, on the "President Harding" for New York. I will see Liveright, look over the proofs of my novel, and then come home. I should be home by the 10th December at the outside. This letter is mainly to explain a cable for money which you *may* get from me. Liveright sent a check, a firm check, and I am having trouble getting it cashed. If I cannot get it cashed here, I'll cable for money and pay it back when I arrive. This is certainly a funny situation to have $200.00 and yet not have it. I may be able to persuade some trusting soul to take it: if not, I'll cable.

I am getting my things together: I have just finished typing 6 short stories which I shall leave with an agent in New York; I have one chapter complete of the Mosquito novel, and almost half of the later one all corrected and typed.[1] I am writing both of them at the same time—a few pages on one tonight, a few pages on the other last night or tomorrow night. You see, I have to do most of my writing at night now, being as I waste nearly the whole day watching the croquet games and the kids playing in the parks. Somehow I have failed to get the cafe habit (every one else in France spends the evening sitting in cafes playing cards or listening to music) Especially the poets. They sit from 6 to 12 o'-clock in rows smoking cigarettes in the cafes, like pigeons on the roof of a barn. But then they've got to spend their time some way, I guess.

Saturday was the anniversary of my widowhood from the P.O. department. I happened to remember it just before I went to sleep, and I spent the entire night hunting for packages, for Dr Swann. (I dont know why Dr Swann.) One nightmare after another.

I kind of got the P.O. mixup by fits and starts. I gather from your last letter that Sonny still has his job, then. I am glad for his sake—knowing Prof Bell slightly.[2] I certainly do crave to hit a golf ball. ~~When you~~ Make the Captain see Dr Rowland or Prof Torrey[3] and engage me for one month, anyway. I will be able to pay that much, and after that the Lord will provide. I was just sitting here supposing, supposing that a fairy would come in and say Well, what'll *you* have? You want something, of course, so get it off your chest. I've got a couple of fur-lined ottomobiles, and here's a man wants ~~an~~ a gardener for his million dollars, and mebbe I got a vacant kingdom or so——And I say right off: Lady, gimme a fresh ham and a medium size big bowl of sweet potatoes, and a trifle or so in the way of buttered cornbread and chocolate pie, and perhaps a little fresh ham much obliged and chocolate pie for dessert, and when that nagging woman has worried me about getting my hair cut until I simply cant stand it anymore, I'll walk out on her and grasp my trusty golf bag, and then Ho for the free and open spaces where its 209 yards to the first green with ~~ten~~ 10% off for Dr Milden.

It still rains—it makes very humid, as we say in France. At home they will see me and say "Why is he so sad looking?" And one replies "Shhh. He spent November in Paris." ~~It's the climate~~ I'm like an Indian chief: Rain in the Face. And behind too, if you aint wrapped up.

Billy

Paris
3 November 1925

[1]*Mosquitoes* was published in 1927; "Elmer" remained unfinished. The six short stories have not been identified.

[2]University postmaster J. W. "Sonny" Bell, Jr. His father, Prof. James Warsaw Bell, was dean of the School of Commerce and Business Administration at the University of Mississippi.

[3]Dr. Peter Whitman Rowland was at one time dean of the University of Mississippi School of Medicine; Robert Torrey was Professor of Mathematics.

To Mrs. M. C. Falkner   9 Nov. 1925
[env]   Paris

I'm having one high and elegant time. With my $200.00 check I go to the American express Co. bank. I stand in line for a long time and then am told I must see the manager. I go to the manager's office: it is 12:30 then, and he is gone to lunch. He returns at 2:15, followed by a train of people all talking at once—like Moses crossing the Red Sea with his gang. After a San Francisco woman gives him hell for 30 minutes, I get to speak to him. Well, he never heard of Boni & Liveright—not a reading man, he explained. He looks in Bradstreet & Dun, Liveright is there, but no rating whatever is given. So he wont take the check.

I have another string to my bow, though; an old Englishman who has lived in Paris a long time and who knows lots of people. He gives me the address of a newspaper man who might help me. I find out in less than 1/2 day that it is the wrong address—the man has moved. I am given the new address, find there a club, but the man himself has gone away. In the meantime, counting on getting my check cashed, I had paid nearly all my money as a deposit on my steamer ticket.

So then I ~~go~~ look in the directory for the Consul's address. The directory reads: Consulates: Voir Annexe administrative. The annexe administrative is not attached to the directory at all, though it is issued quite often. They didn't have one there, however, so I went to a cop. He had a little book that told when the last French king died and how high the Arc de Triomphe is and what streets meet at the Place d'l Opera, but it hadn't heard of the American Consul. I knew where the Embassy was though, so I went there, and got the Consul's address from them. And got quite courteously turned down once more. So there I was, with $200.00 and not 50 francs to bless myself with.

This morning I rose, determined. It is a well-known fact in Europe that, when you are in trouble, regardless of nationality, ~~the~~ go to the British Consul—he will always help you. That's why they are the greatest nation on earth, even if the Empire is dying. So I had started there when I received a letter from Phil with $25.00 in it. So now I am all right. The check will have to go to New York, then return.

So the chances are I shall miss the boat on the 19th. If I do, I shant sail until Dec. 2nd. Be home Xmas, anyway.

Billy

Nov 9 1925

To Mrs. M. C. Falkner 15 Nov. 1925
[postcard] 543 Nos Bouquinistes—LL
Paris

Still hoping to get the boat on the 19th. If not, I think I can get one on the 25th. I'll sure be glad when I get off—this is Saint Martin's summer, I have seen ice every morning for a week, and yesterday it snowed. Good thing the Lord gave these folks wine—they rate a recompense of some kind for this climate.

Billy

Nov 15, 1925

To Mrs. M. C. Falkner 21 Nov. 1925
Paris

The advice for my check has not been returned. They ~~tod~~ told me the 18th: it is now the 21st. Which means that I will miss the Leviathan which sails Tuesday, and the next boat sails Dec. 2. I will take that—provided of course that I get my money by then. I have never prepared a speech in my life, but I've sure got one for Mr Horace Liveright. Sending me, a stranger in a foreign land 2000 miles away, a personal check! If it hadn't been for a photographer whom I know and who is almost as poor as I am, I'd have starved to death. By sailing the 19th, I'd have been able to buy some Xmas presents here, but having to wait until the 2-December, I just will get home. But enough of this: the more I think about it the madder I get. A check for $200.00 mind you, and not a sou to buy Jimmy a toy wagon with. I'm sure to get it by the end of the month, however: I expect it Monday, when it is too late to get a ticket for the Leviathan. At this rate, I'll be home about Dec 15th. Damn that Jew.

Cold as time: stays below freezing all day long. I have got used to it, though, ~~what~~ my new suit is quite heavy and well-lined. My poor trench coat is about gone, though. I am going to put it away when I get home, with a widow's pension. The kids here dont seem to mind the cold at all— outdoors all day long. They are awful cute: bundled up so that they can hardly move, and when they fall they can neither get their hands out of their pockets nor get up again without help. They wear leather leggings, but between the tops of the leggings and their drawers is nothing but bare pink skin.

I've been too upset to do any more on my novel, but I am writing another short story. This will make 7 for the agent in New York: money to buy an overcoat with.

I had a letter from Ben Wasson[1] this week. My beard is quite elegant: it is trimmed to a point now. Swell.

I will sail the 2 Dec. *Provided.* O *damn* that jew.

Billy

21 Nov 1925

---

[1]Ben Wasson, from Greenville, Mississippi, was a member of Sigma Alpha Epsilon

fraternity with Faulkner at the University of Mississippi, 1919–1920, and served as his
sometime literary agent during the 1920s and 1930s.

To Mrs. M. C. Falkner   30 Nov. 1925
[env]   Paris

Nov 30, the advice for the check has not come yet. So I miss
the boat on Dec 2. So I have no idea when I will get home.
Had I only known this was to come about, I'd have kept the
check, gone to a sea-port and tried to work my passage
across. But the people at the bank assured me it would take
only eight days. It has been 24 days. And I owe my landlady
too much rent now, to skip out. I'll just have to cool my
heels until the advice for the check comes. What makes me
so mad is having to stay in a city, a land I'm tired off, having
to spend money I dont want to spend, knowing I'll probably
not get home for Xmas, and having my mind so fretted I
cant write anything worth 8 whoops. I've even read all the
books I brought with me at least 5 times.

While I think of it—*Do Not try to send me any money
without a request from me.* My money is liable to come any
day, and I am going away from Paris within 3 days of its
arrival, and to cable money is expensive, too much so to
have it arrive after my departure. When I get my $200.00 I
will liquidate all right—I wont need any more than that. So
dont try to send money unless I cable for it.

                                                            Billy

30 Nov 1925

To Mr. M. C. Falkner   19 Dec. 1925
[telegram]   New York
                                              2:32 P.M.

LANDED TODAY¹ WIRE FIFTY DOLLARS CARE HOTEL PENNSYLVANIA
HOME WEDNESDAY

[t] Billy

¹Faulkner sailed from Cherbourg on December 9 aboard the S.S. *Republic*.

To Mrs. M. C. Falkner   [postmarked 21 Dec. 1925]
[env]   Hotel Pennsylvania
                                    New York

Dear Moms—

   I will have to stay here and get the novel proofs straightened out. I will not get home Wednesday, but I am doing my darndest to make it by Thursday.

   Liveright will not be in town until tomorrow. Love to everybody

Billy

Census

William Faulkner's Letters
to His Mother and Father
1912, 1918–1925

Page numbers (first column) and dates (third column) in the Census accord with those in the text. The physical form of each letter is given in the second column by the following abbreviations: AL (autograph letter unsigned), ALS (autograph letter signed), APCS (autograph post-card signed), TL (typed letter unsigned), TLS (typed letter signed), TLTS (typed letter typed signature), Tel. (telegram). The letters are written in ink or pencil, or typed on a black or purple ribbon as indicated. Dates in the third column are given in brackets when not inscribed on the letters; dates not given in full in the letters have been determined from envelope postmarks and/or internal evidence. Salutations in the fourth column employ the abbreviations D. (Dear) and d. (dear). Information from envelopes includes addressees, abbreviated Mrs MC (Maud Falkner), Mr MC (Murry Falkner), places of origin, and postmarks. Names of addressees starred in the July to December 1918 letters (Mrs MC*) indicate that the surname is spelled Faulkner, with a "u." Missing dates, salutations, and/or envelopes are indicated by a dash (—).

		Date	Salutation	Envelope/ Origin/ Postmark
	August 1912			
39	ALS ink	8-16-12	D. Miss Lady	—
	April to June 1918			
44	ALS ink	Fri [5]	D. Lady	Mrs MC New Haven 4-5-18
46	ALS ink	Sat [6]	D. Dad	Mr MC New Haven 4-6-18

		Date	Salutation	Envelope/ Origin/ Postmark
47	ALS ink	Sat [6]	Darling Momsey	Mrs MC New Haven 4-7-18
48	AL ink	Sun [7] 8 PM	D. Mother and Dad	Mr MC New Haven 4-7-18
49	AL ink	Tue [9]	D. Momsey	Mrs MC New Haven 4-9-18
50	ALS ink	Sun [14]	—	Mrs MC New Haven 4-14-18
51	ALS ink	Sun [21]	—	Mrs MC New Haven 4-22-18
52	ALS ink	Wed [4-24-18]	D. Mother and Dad	—
54	AL ink	Sun [4-28-18]	Darling Momsey	—
55	AL ink	—	D. Mother	Mrs MC New Haven 5-5-18
56	ALS ink	Sun [19]	—	Mrs MC New Haven 5-20-18
58	ALS ink	—	—	Mrs MC New Haven 5-27-18
59	ALS ink	[Thu, 30]	My d. Lady	—
61	ALS pencil	Sun [2]	D. Mother	Mrs MC New Haven 6-2-18
63	ALS ink	—	Darling Momsy and Dad	Mrs MC New Haven 6-7-18

		Date	Salutation	Envelope/ Origin/ Postmark
64	ALS ink	Thu [13] 8 PM	Dearest Mother	Mrs MC New Haven 6-13-18

July to December 1918

		Date	Salutation	Envelope/ Origin/ Postmark
71	ALS pencil	Mon [8] 10AM	—	Mrs MC New York 7-8-18
72	Tel	7-8-18 NY/NY 2:30 PM	—	Mrs MC
72	APCS ink	—	—	Mrs MC Albany NY 7-8-18
72	ALS ink	Toronto Tue [9]	Darling Mother	Mrs MC* Toronto 7-9-18 6:30 PM
74	ALS ink	—	D. Mother and Dad	Mrs MC* Toronto 7-9-18 9:30 PM
75	ALS pencil	—	—	Mrs MC* Toronto 7-10-18
76	ALS pencil	Thu [11]	—	Mrs MC* Toronto 7-12-18
77	ALS pencil	Sat [13]	Mother darling	Mrs MC* Toronto 7-15-18
78	ALS pencil	Mon [15] 10:30 AM	D. Mother	Mrs MC* Toronto 7-15-18
79	ALS pencil	Tue [16]	D. Mother	Mrs MC* Toronto 7-17-18

		Date	Salutation	Envelope/ Origin/ Postmark
80	ALS ink	Fri [19]	D. Mother and Dad	Mrs MC* Toronto 7-[20]-18
82	ALS ink	Mon [22] 5:30	D. Mother	Mrs MC* Toronto 7-23-18
83	ALS ink	Tue [23]	—	Mrs MC* Toronto 7-25-18
84	ALS ink	Wed [24]	—	Mrs MC* Toronto 7-25-18
84	ALS pencil	Sun [28]	D. Mother and Dad	Mrs MC* Long Branch 7-28-18
86	AL pencil	"?"	D. Mother	Mrs MC* Long Branch 7-31-18
86	ALS pencil	Wed [31]	D. Mother and Dad	Mrs MC* Long Branch 8-1-18
87	ALS pencil	Sat [3]	D. Mother and Dad	Mrs MC* Long Branch 8-4-18
88	ALS pencil	Sat [10] PM	—	Mrs MC* Long Branch 8-10-18
89	ALS pencil/ink	Sun [11]	Mother and Dad	Mrs MC* Long Branch 8-12-18

		Date	Salutation	Envelope/ Origin/ Postmark
90	AL pencil	Mon [12]	Mother Darling	Mrs MC* Long Branch 8-13-18
92	AL pencil	Thu [15]	—	Mrs MC* Long Branch 8-19-18
93	ALS pencil	Sun [18]	D. Mother and Dad	Mrs MC* Long Branch 8-19-18
94	AL pencil	Thu [22]	—	Mrs MC* Long Branch 8-23-18
95	ALS pencil	Tue [27]	—	Mrs MC* Long Branch 8-29-18
96	ALS pencil	Fri [30]	—	Mrs MC* Long Branch 8-30-18
97	AL pencil	Sun 1–18	—	Mrs MC* Long Branch 9-3-18
98	ALS pencil	Thu [5]	D. Mother and Dad	Mrs MC* Long Branch 9-5-18
99	AL pencil	Mon [9]	—	Mrs MC* Long Branch [9-10-18]

		Date	Salutation	Envelope/ Origin/ Postmark
100	ALS pencil	Thu 12	D. Mother and Dad	Mrs MC* Long Branch 9-14-18
102	ALS ink/pencil	Sun [15]	—	Mrs MC* Long Branch 9-16-18
103	ALS pencil	Tue [17]	—	Mrs MC* Long Branch 9-17-18
104	ALS pencil	Thu [19]	—	Mrs MC* Long Branch 9-19-18
105	ALS pencil	Sat [21]	D. Mother	Mrs MC* Toronto 9-22-18
106	ALS pencil	Mon [23]	—	Mrs MC* Toronto 9-24-18
107	ALS pencil	Wed [25]	D. Mother and Dad	Mrs MC* Toronto 9-25-18
108	ALS pencil	Sat 28	D. Mother and Dad	Mrs MC* Toronto 9-28-18
109	ALS pencil	Thu [3]	D. Mother and Dad	Mrs MC* Toronto 10-4-18
111	ALS pencil	Sun [6]	—	Mrs MC* Toronto 10-6-18
112	ALS pencil	Thu [10] 11:00 AM	—	Mrs MC* Toronto 10-10-18

		Date	Salutation	Envelope/ Origin/ Postmark
114	ALS pencil	Sun [13]	—	Mrs MC Toronto 10-14-18
115	ALS ink	Mon [14]	D. Madam	Mrs MC* Toronto 10-15-18
116	ALS pencil	Thu [17]	Mother Darling	Mrs MC Toronto 10-18-18
117	ALS ink	Mon [21]	—	Mrs MC* Toronto 10-21-18
119	AL ink	Thu [24]	D. Mother	Mrs MC* Toronto 10-24-18
120	ALS ink	Fri [25]	Mother Darling	Mrs MC Toronto 10-26-18
121	ALS ink	Mon [28]	—	Mrs MC* Toronto 10-29-18
121	ALS ink	Wed [30]		Mrs MC Toronto 10-30-18
122	ALS ink	Thu 31	Momsey dear	Mrs MC Toronto 11-1-18
123	AL ink	Sun [3]	—	Mrs MC Toronto 11-3-18
125	ALS ink	Tue [5]	Mother darling	Mrs MC Toronto 11-6-18
126	ALS ink	Thu [7] Sat [9]	D. Momsey	Mrs MC Toronto 11-9-18

		Date	Salutation	Envelope/ Origin/ Postmark
128	ALS ink	Sun [10]	Mother and Dad	Mrs MC* Toronto 11-11-18
129	ALS ink	Wed [13] Fri [15]	D. Mother	Mrs MC* Toronto 11-16-18
130	ALS ink	Sun [17]	Mother Dear	Mrs MC* Toronto 11-18-18
131	ALS ink	Tue [19]	D. Mother and Dad	Mrs MC* Toronto 11-[21]-18
133	ALS ink	Fri [22]	Mother darling	Mrs MC Toronto 11-22-18
135	ALS ink	Sun [24]	D. Mother and Dad	Mrs MC Toronto 10:30 AM 11-25-18
136	Tel	11-24/25-18 Toronto 8:11 PM	D. Dad	Mr MC
136	ALS ink	Thu [28]	Darling Mother	Mrs MC Toronto 11-29-18
137	ALS ink	Sat [30]	D. Momsey	Mrs MC Toronto 12-1-18
138	ALS ink	Wed 4	D. Mother	Mrs MC* Toronto 12-6-18
139	Tel	12-9-18 Cinninati 5:00 PM	—	Mrs MC*

		Date	Salutation	Envelope/ Origin/ Postmark
	October to December 1921			
144	ALS ink	Thu [6] New Haven	—	Mrs MC New Haven 10-7-21
146	ALS ink	Sun [9]	D. Mother	Mrs MC New Haven 10-9-21
147	ALS ink	Thu [13]	D. Mother	Mrs MC New Haven 10-13-21
148	ALS ink/pencil	Mon [17]	D. Dad	Mr MC New Haven 10-17-21
150	AL ink	Thu [20]	D. Mother	Mrs MC New Haven 10-20-21
151	ALS ink	Tue [25]	D. Mother	Mrs MC New Haven 10-27-21
154	ALS ink	Sat [29]	—	Mrs MC New Haven 10-29-21
154	ALS ink	—	—	Mrs MC New Haven 11-1-21
155	ALS ink	—	—	Mrs MC New York 11-10-21
158	AL ink	—	D. Mother	Mrs MC New York 11-12-21
160	ALS ink	—	D. Mother	Mrs MC New York 11-16-21

		Date	*Salutation*	*Envelope/ Origin/ Postmark*
161	ALS ink	Sun [20]	D. Sweetness	Mr Dean Falkner New York 11-21-21
162	ALS ink	—	D. Moms	Mrs MC New York 11-23-21

January to July 1925

169	ALS ink	6 January 192[5]	D. Mother	—
170	ALS ink	[early Jan]	D. Mother	—
172	ALS ink	Mon [12]	D. Mother	—
173	ALS ink	[mid-Jan]	D. Mother	—
175	ALS ink	[mid-Jan]	D. Mother	—
176	TLTS black ribbon	Thu [22]	—	Mrs MC New Orleans 1-22-25
178	ALS ink	—	—	Mrs MC New Orleans 1-27-25
178	ALS ink	[late Jan]	D. Mother	—
179	ALS ink	[early Feb]	D. Mother	—
180	ALS ink	[early Feb]	D. Mother	—
181	TLS black ribbon	[7 Feb]	D. Mother	—
183	TLS black ribbon	[early Feb]	D. Moms	—
184	ALS ink	[16 Feb]	—	—
185	TL black ribbon	Fri [20]	—	Mrs MC New Orleans 2-20-25
185	ALS ink	[28 Feb] [Memphis]	D. Mother	—

		Date	Salutation	Envelope/ Origin/ Postmark
186	ALS ink	—	D. Mother	Mrs. MC New Orleans 3-3-25
186	ALS ink	—	D. Mother	Mrs MC New Orleans 3-5-25
187	TLTS black ribbon	[early Mar]	D. Mother	—
188	ALS ink	—	—	Mrs MC New Orleans 3-8-25
189	ALS ink	—	D. Mother and Dad	Mrs MC New Orleans 3-11-25
190	TLTS black ribbon	—	D. Mother	Mrs MC New Orleans 3-18-25
191	TLTS black ribbon	[late Mar]	D. Mother	—
194	TLTS black ribbon	—	D. Mother	Mrs MC New Orleans 3-26-25
194	TLTS black ribbon	—	D. Mother	Mrs MC New Orleans 3-31-25
195	TLTS purple ribbon	[early Apr]	D. Mother	—
197	TLTS purple ribbon	—	Moms, dear heart	Mrs MC New Orleans 4-7-25
198	TLTS purple ribbon	—	Dear Moms	Mrs MC New Orleans 4-10-25
198	encl. TcarbonLS	—	Dear Mr Little	—

		Date	Salutation	Envelope/ Origin/ Postmark
199	TLTS purple ribbon	—	D. Mother	Mrs MC New Orleans 4-13-25
200	TLTS purple ribbon		D. Mother	Mrs MC New Orleans 4-16-25
201	TL purple ribbon	—	D. Moms	Mrs MC New Orleans 4-20-25
203	TLTS purple ribbon	—	D. Moms	Mrs MC New Orleans 4-23-25
204	TLTS purple ribbon	—	D. Moms	Mrs MC New Orleans 5-1-25
206	TLTS purple ribbon	[early May]	D. Moms	—
207	TLTS purple ribbon	—	D. Moms	Mrs MC New Orleans 5-7-25
208	TLTS purple ribbon	—	D. Moms	Mrs MC New Orleans 5-12-25
209	TLTS purple ribbon	[mid-May]	D. Moms	—
209	ALS ink	—	D. Moms	Mrs MC New Orleans 6-1-25
210	AL ink	—	—	Mrs MC New Orleans 6-11-25
211	ALS ink	—	D. Moms	Mrs MC Pascagoula 6-22-25

		Date	Salutation	Envelope/ Origin/ Postmark
211	ALS ink	—	D. Moms	Mrs MC Pascagoula 6-25-25
212	ALS ink	[early July]	D. Moms	—
213	TLTS black ribbon	Mon [6] 11:00 AM	D. Moms	Mrs MC New Orleans 7-7-25

October to December 1925

		Date	Salutation	Envelope/ Origin/ Postmark
218	TLS black ribbon	10-17-25 Paris	D. Dad	Mr MC Paris 10-17-25
219	ALS ink	10-21-25 Paris	D. Moms	Mrs MC Paris 10-21-25
222	ALS ink	10-26-25	—	Mrs MC Paris 10-26-25
223	ALS ink	10-30-25 Paris	D. Moms	Mrs MC Paris 10-31-25
224	ALS ink	11-3-25 Paris	D. Moms	Mrs MC Paris 11-4-25
226	ALS ink	11-9-25	—	Mrs MC Paris 11-9-25
228	APCS ink	11-15-25	—	Mrs MC Paris 11-16-25
228	ALS ink	11-21-25	—	Mrs MC Paris 11-22-25
230	ALS ink	11-30-25	—	Mrs MC Paris 11-30-25

		Date	*Salutation*	*Envelope/ Origin/ Postmark*
231	Tel	12-19-15 NY/NY 1:57 PM	—	Mr MC
231	ALS ink	—	D. Moms	Mrs MC New York 12-21-25

Index